J.M. Keynes' Theory of Decision Making, Induction, and Analogy

J.M. Keynes' Theory of Decision Making, Induction, and Analogy

The Role of Interval Valued Probability in His Approach

MICHAEL EMMETT BRADY

To order additional copies of this book, contact:
Xlibris Corporation
1-888-795-4274
www.Xlibris.com
Orders@Xlibris.com
26218

CONTENTS

Dedicated To

My Late Relatives,

Mary Alice Bye

and

Richard Ryan

Acknowledgments

I want to thank the Father, Son, and Holy Spirit and/or their angels for inspiration, understanding, guidance, and patience.

I also thank my parents, Emmett Merchant Brady and Bernadette Loch Brady, who provided me with the intellectual tools and appreciation for scholarly work without which this book would have been impossible to write.

Finally, I thank Cindy Barr for her excellent word processing of the manuscript.

Introduction

This book is an abridged version of my *Essays On J.M. Keynes* (2004) that concentrates on issues of probability, induction, analogy, and decision making. It contains one new essay, essay 4. This essay demonstrates that the economics and philosophy professions' assessment of Keynes' *A Treatise on Probability* (TP) is fatally flawed, due to their total reliance on misinformed book reviews done by F. Ramsey. All of the technical work done by Keynes in Parts 2 and 3 of the TP is ignored, especially Keynes' work on interval estimates and finite probabilities.

1

Keynes, Mathematics, and Probability:

A Reappraisal

1. Introduction

I n the half century that has passed since J.M. Keynes wrote "A Treatise on Probability" (TP) and "The General Theory" (GT), two beliefs have taken hold among economists. The first concerns Keynes' own mathematical, logical and analytic capabilities and competence. It is widely believed that Keynes provided no rigorous foundation, in fact, no foundation at all, in microeconomic theory for his "Theory of Effective Demand". A corollary to this first belief is that Keynes simply lacked the necessary mathematical training in microeconomics. Hence, the GT is a logical and mathematical maze or quagmire of pretentious symbols and inappropriate definitions.[1] Surprisingly, this belief first appears to have taken root among Keynes' alleged circle of admirers at Cambridge, England.[2] I cover this belief, which has by now become accepted "fact", in section 7 below.

The second belief will require five sections to treat. This second belief conjectures that Keynes realized, starting early in his career, that the use of logical, mathematical and statistical methods in the social sciences in general, and economics, in particular, were inappropriate and unsuitable, due to the type of phenomena studied. Supposedly, this view can be clearly traced starting with Keynes' TP, through his "Essays in Biography" (EB), and GT, to his 1937 *Quarterly Journal of Economics* (QJE) article, where this belief is supposedly presented in its most mature form. The next four section of the paper will demonstrate that this is not the case. The rest of this section will be used to illustrate Keynes' approach to the use of numbers in any kind of formal analysis.

Keynes was a lifelong opponent of the use of what today statisticians call "point estimates". Point estimates are *single* number answers to statistical and mathematical probability problems. Instead, Keynes was a proponent of what are today called "interval estimates", as well as ordinal comparisons or rankings. It is in the Tolerance Limits of non-parametric, distribution free, statistical approaches, or in the Confidence Intervals of parametric, classical statistical approaches, that one finds such interval estimates. Unfortunately, non-parametric approaches were not formally developed until 1946, while the parametric approach did not formally, in the literature, discuss interval estimates for the first time until 1932. Keynes was writing at a time when all of his academic opponents were point estimate practitioners.

Keynes called his general approach to interval estimation his "inexact numerical comparison" approach (chapter 5, 15, and 17 of the TP), or his "inexact numerical approximation" technique (chapters 15 and 17 of the TP). This approximation technique is then applied in chapters 20, 25, 29 and 30 of the TP. Keynes' method is based directly on George Boole's Boolean Logic which Boole then showed could be applied to problems in algebra and probability. In Boole's "The Laws of Thought" (LT), the first 10 chapters develop the logic, while chapters 11-15 apply it to algebra and chapters 16-21 apply it to probability. Keynes improved upon some aspects of Boole's analytic technique and used it to calculate least upper bound (l.u.b.) and greatest lower bound (g.l.b.) probability estimates. For example, Keynes' major result for pure induction, contained in chapter 20 of the TP (1921, pp. 235-36), is an extension of Boole's problem x, contained on pp. 357-359 of the LT. Keynes reformulated Boole's analysis in an improved version on pp. 192-194 of the TP.

Yet Boole's method disappeared from general usage after the TP was published. It was just too difficult to master. Yet it is exactly this technique which Keynes wanted to substitute for methods based on the assumption of equiprobable outcomes for some cases. Keynes' problems numbered 51 through 58, from pp. 162-194 of the TP, are worked out in complete detail. All that is required is some familiarity with Boole's original approach and a lot of time, as Keynes skips many steps.

Thus, I will argue that when Keynes states that, in general, probabilities are not susceptible to numerical estimation, he is arguing that the probabilities, in general, can't be represented by single number answers or point estimates. *But* they can be represented by intervals. In the next four sections all underscores are the author's, not Keynes', unless stated.

2. What did Keynes say in the TP?

"For this purpose it would only encumber the exposition, without adding to its clearness or its accuracy, if I were to employ the *perfectly exact* terminology . . . necessary for the avoidance of error . . . While taking pains, therefore, to avoid any divergence between the substance of this chapter and of those which succeed it, and to employ only such paraphrases as could be translated, if desired, into *perfectly exact language.*" (Keynes, 1921, p. 18)

Keynes continues in a footnote:

". . . There are occasions for *very exact methods* of statement, such as are employed in Mr. Russell's Principia Mathematic . . . Mr. Moore has developed in Principia Ethica an *intermediate* style . . . But those writers, who strain after *exaggerated precision* . . . lose the readers attention . . . without their really attaining . . . a *complete precision*", (Keynes, 1921, p. 19).

Keynes continues throughout the TP to make the above distinction:

> "... it is evident that judgments based on a somewhat indefinite experience of the past do not easily lend themselves to *precise* numerical appraisement", (Keynes, 1921, p. 81).
>
> "No other formula (i.e. Principle of Indifference) in the alchemy of logic has exerted more astonishing powers. For it has established the existence of God from the premise of total ignorance, and it has measured with *numerical precision* the probability that the sun will rise tomorrow", (Keynes, 1921, p. 82).
>
> "I argued in chapter III that not all probabilities have an *exact numerical value* . . . we can sometimes compare a non-numerical probability in respect of more or less with one of these numerical probabilities. This enables us to give a definition of 'finite probability' which is capable of application to non-numerical, as well as numerical, probabilities. I define 'finite probability' as on which exceeds some numerical probability", (Keynes, 1921, p. 237).

We will see at the end of this section that Savage's method of eliciting numerical subjective probabilities involves much that same process of comparing the non-specified subjectives probability models or the knowledge of "expert" opinion. The difference between Keynes and Savage were first, Savage refused to model mathematically "vagueness" or "ambiguity" and second, that Savage would continue the process of comparison until point estimates were obtained,[3] a goal Keynes would reject as not possible.

> "Common sense tells us some inductive arguments are stronger than others . . . The probability of an induction is only *numerically definite* when we are able to make definite assumptions about the number of independent equiprobable influences at work. *Otherwise*, it is non-numerical, though bearing relations of greater or less to numerical probabilities according to the *approximate limits*

with which our assumptions as to the possible number of these causes lie", (Keynes, 1921, p. 259).

Thus,

The hope, which sustained many investigators . . . of gradually bringing the moral sciences under the sway of mathematical reasoning, steadily recedes—*if we mean, as they meant, by mathematics, the introduction of precise numerical methods* . . . Mathematical reasoning now appears as an aid in its symbolic rather than its numerical character". (Keynes, 1921, p. 316).

A brief degression into differential equations will demonstrate Keynes' point. Only first or second order constant coefficient, homogenous, linear or exact differential equations can be solved for a precise numerical answer. A few other types, like the Bessel equation, can be solved by series expansion. Almost all non-linear differential equations can't be solved, in general. However, the qualitative phase diagram approach can let the scientist know in which region or area of the diagram a solution may lie, given the initial conditions. Thus, no precise numerical answer is calculatable.

We will now follow Keynes in explicitly differentiating numerical (point) estimates from non-numerical (interval) estimates.

Thus,

"We are able, I think, always to compare a pair of probabilities which are

(i.) of the type ab/h and a/h,

or

(ii.) of the type a/hh_1 and a/h, provided the additional evidence, h_1, contains only one independent piece of relevant information," (Keynes, 1921, p. 65).

"Other comparisons are possibly by a combination of these two principles with the Principle of Indifference," (Keynes, 1921, p. 66).

"Category (ii) is very wide, and evidently covers a great
variety of cases," (Keynes, 1921, p. 68).

Keynes' conclusion is very clear:

"The sphere of inexact numerical calculation is not,
however, quite so limited. Many probabilities, which are
incapable of numerical measurement, *can be placed between*
(Keynes' underscore) numerical limits. And by taking
particular non-numerical probabilities as standards a great
number of comparisons or approximate measurements
become possible. If we can place a probability in an order of
magnitude with some standard probability, we can obtain
its approximate measure by comparison.
This method is frequently adopted in common
discourse," (Keynes 1921, p. 160).

It was also adopted by Savage, as we have seen. In conclusion,
Keynes believed that "*perfectly* equal probabilities, and hence *exact*
numerical measures, will occur comparatively seldom", (Keynes, 1921,
p. 160). However, Keynes did not conclude from this what has been
claimed as Keynes' position, that Keynes was opposed to the use of
mathematics and/or statistics. On the contrary, the mathematics
Keynes felt appropriate, given the indefinite state of information, was
his inexact (interval estimate) numerical comparison approach,
illustrated in its most demanding form as an application of Boolean
algebra in chapters 15 and 17 of the TP. Keynes also provided the
reader with his "conventional coefficient of risk and weight" in chapter
26 as well as recommending the use of Chebyshev's Inequality in
order to calculate imprecise numerical answers in chapter 30.

3. What can we learn by way of Keynes' evaluations of Ramsey and Edgeworth?

In his EB, Keynes evaluated both Ramsey and Edgeworth.
Ramsey was praised. Edgeworth was found wanting. This was due
to Ramsey's use of advanced mathematics to obtain applicable

qualitative results, while Edgeworth was obsessed with precise exact numerical answers. First, we present Keynes' views on Ramsey:

> "But he has left behind him in print . . . only two witnesses to his powers—his papers published in the Economic Journal . . . in March, 1927 . . . and . . . in December, 1928. The latter of these is, I think, one of the most remarkable contributions to mathematical economics ever made, both in respect of the *intrinsic importance* and difficulty of its subject, the *power* and elegance of the *technical methods* employed, and the clear purity of illumination . . . The article is terribly difficult reading for an economist, but it is not difficult to appreciate how *scientific* and aesthetic qualities are combined in it together," (CWJMK, 1973, Vol. 10, pp. 335-36).

I am unaware of any other commentator on Keynes' views on mathematics who has ever mentioned Keynes' comment on Ramsey, except for an irrelevant conclusion by Samuelson (1946, p. 202, ft. 8).

Why was Keynes so impressed with this work of applied mathematics? The answer is that Ramsey demonstrated that a short run, maximizing approach, represented by a high rate of discount, led to insufficient investment and hence secular stagnation for the economy as a whole. For Keynes, Ramsey's paper translated as "A mathematical theory of consumption and investment". Yet in this same selection, Keynes also mentions that the continued development of pure formal logic has led "gradually to empty it of content and to reduce it more and more to mere dry bones, until finally it seemed to exclude not only all experience but most of the principles, usually reckoned logical, of reasonable thought", (CWJMK, Vol.10, p. 338). Keynes agrees with Ramsey's opposition to this trend. Thus, "Ramsey may have been pointing the way to the next field of study when formal logic has been put into good order and its highly limited scope properly defined," (CWJMK, Vol. 10, p. 339). However, Keynes' recognition of the highly limited scope of pure formal symbolic logic does not translate or support the supposition that mathematics in general also suffers from such a limitation. Formal logic is only one very small part of mathematics.

In section 5 of chapter 25 of the TP, Keynes devotes pages 298-302 to an examination of psychical research in general, Edgeworth's in particular. Keynes concludes, exactly contrary to Edgeworth, that

> ". . . we should be very chary of applying to problems of psychical research the calculus. The alternatives seldom satisfy the conditions for the application of the Principle of Indifference, and the initial probabilities are not capable of being measured numerically," (Keynes, 1921, p. 302).

Keynes' later views of Edgeworth's attempts at applying the Benthamite Utilitarian "point estimate" calculus to every field in sight are no different from the assessment above or on p. 316 of the TP (also see CWJMK, Vol. 10, pp. 254-262). It is important to notice that Keynes called Edgeworth's attempts at applying exact or precise numerical calculation techniques "quasi-mathematical". In Keynes' view, Edgeworth lacked the mathematical sophistication of a Poincare, who was aware of the problems that, "We are faced at every time . . . of discreteness, of discontinuity-the whole is not equal to the sum of the parts . . . small changes produce large effects, the assumptions of a uniform and homogeneous continuum are not satisfied," (Keynes 1923, Vol. 10, p. 262). Also see Keynes, 1921, pp. 48-49, 84, 284-86, 289 for his positive assessments of Poincare's work. Recently, Poincare's initial and original analysis of non-linear differential equations has been revived under the name Chaos Theory.[4]

It turns out that Keynes had a very high degree of mathematical sophistication. The quote above demonstrates that Keynes had, like Poincare, recognized the importance of non-linearity in the world. Keynes would easily fit into the field of modern chaos research with his ideas.

In summary, Keynes praised Ramsey's use of the variational calculus to obtain sound qualitative results through the application of the non-linear Euler Lagrange equation. Keynes damned Edgeworth's varied attempts at applying classical linear mathematical and statistical techniques to areas of study where Keynes felt the data only allowed qualitative results to be attained. Edgeworth's attempt to model all social phenomena in such a way as to attain a unique number answer was regarded by Keynes as the height of folly.

4. What did Keynes say in the GT?

"Since, therefore, real income in terms of product, may be incapable of *precise numerical* measurement, it is often convenient to regard income in terms of wage units . . .," (Keynes, 1964, p. 114).

"Our normal psychological law . . . can therefore be translated—not, indeed, *with absolute accuracy* but subject to qualifications which are obvious and can easily be stated in a formally complete fashion," (Keynes, 1964, p. 114).

"Most probably, of our decisions to do something positive . . . can only be taken as a result . . . of a spontaneous urge to action rather than inaction, and not as the outcome of a weighted average of quantitative benefits multiplied by quantitative probabilities . . . . Only a little more than an expedition to the South Pole, is it [Enterprise] based on an *exact* calculation of benefits to come . . . But individual initiative will only be adequate when *reasonable calculation* is supplemented and supported by animal spirits . . . We are merely reminding ourselves that human decisions affecting the future . . . cannot depend on *strict mathematical expectation*, since the basis for making such calculations does not exist . . .," (Keynes, 1964, pp. 161-163).

"The *actuarial* profit or mathematical expectation of gain calculated in accordance with the existing probabilities—if it can be so calculated, which is doubtful," (Keynes, 1964, p. 169).

Again, Keynes is arguing against the use of precise, exact or strict mathematical expectation calculations. In other words, point estimates. By "reasonable calculation", Keynes means the use of his "non-numerical" inexact numerical approximation[5] approach.

Keynes also made some general comments on the role of mathematics in scientific methodology, as applied to economics:

> "The object of our analyses is . . . to provide ourselves
> with an organized . . . method of thinking our particular
> problems; and, after we have reached a provisional
> conclusion by isolating the complicating factors one by one,
> we then . . . allow for the probable interactions . . . This is
> the nature of economic thinking. Any other way of applying
> our formal principles of thought . . . will lead us to error. It is
> great fault of symbolic *pseudo*-mathematical methods of
> formalizing a system of economic analysis . . . that they
> expressly assume strict independence between the factors
> involved and lose all their cogency and authority if this
> hypothesis is disallowed.", (Keynes, 1964, p. 297).

Thus,

> "Too large a proportion of recent '*mathematical*'
> economics are mere concoctions, as imprecise as the initial
> assumptions they rest on, which allow the author to lose
> sight of the complexities and interdependencies of the real
> world in a maze of pretentious and unhelpful symbols",
> (Keynes, 1964, p. 298).

These two quotations, along with a similar quotation from p. 275 of the GT, have been widely quoted and horribly misinterpreted. Keynes' objection, on both p. 275 and pp. 297-98 of the GT, is to pseudo-mathematical methods, which ignore feedback and interactive effects and assume strict independence among the variables. Obviously, such assumptions would lead to simple, unrealistic *linear* models. Keynes, on the other hand, was simply more advanced in his understanding of the need to model such economic phenomenon *non-linearly*. Since such models can't be quantitatively solved, except under very special conditions, correct qualitative results, and not quantitative point estimates, are the goal of economic science.

5. What did Keynes say after the G.T.?

> "But at any given time facts and expectations were assumed to be given in a definite and calculable form; and risks, of which, though admitted, not much notice was taken, were supposed to be capable of an *exact actuarial computation* . . . just as in the Benthamite calculus of pain and pleasure . . . by which the Benthamite philosophy assumed men to be influenced . . .", (Keynes, 1973, p. 213).
>
> "The orthodox theory assumes that we have a knowledge of the future of a kind quite different from that we actually possess. This false rationalization follows the lines of the *Benthamite* calculus", (Keynes, 1937, p. 222).

There is nothing being said here that Keynes did not already say, for instance, in much greater detail in the TP (see Keynes, 1921, pp. 309, 316). Unfortunately, Keynes does not point out that he is not opposed to the use of numbers, only their misuse as point estimates, in this essay. However, since he had discussed his inexact approach or applied it in ten chapters in the TP (chapters 5, 10, 14, 15-17, 20, 25, 29-30), his omission is understandable. In conclusion, I find absolutely no textual evidence to support the claim, made in the following two sections, that Keynes was either opposed to the use of mathematical methods or that he himself was ignorant and error prone in the use of such methods.[6] Instead, I find a mathematical sophistication 60 years ahead of his time.

6. Was Keynes opposed to the "mathematical method"?

> "Keynes' uneasiness with 'mathematical psychics' had a profound effect on his vision of economics. The application

of mathematical methods to the social sciences did not yield
the definitive results that it availed to physics", (Rotheim,
1989-90, p. 320).

Continuing, Rotheim states:

"What did this imply for Keynes? First, the economic
world was much more complex and uncertain than the
world of physics (?—author's query), and attempting to
model such a world would be next to impossible. Second,
such a mathematical approach is deceptive, because it forces
the economist to think within the confines of the
mathematical method itself; and this greatly narrows the
nature and method of economic research. In the "General
Theory" Keynes referred to this approach in terms of 'The
pitfalls of a pseudo-mathematical method . . . ' Keynes
believed this method to be inapplicable to the economic
world . . .", (Rotheim, 1989-90, p. 320).

"In the "General Theory", Keynes finds the assumption
of independence of elements assumed by the mathematical
method to be misdirected and inappropriate", (Rotheim,
op. cit., p. 320).

Rotheim then proceeds to give the p. 275 and pp. 297-98
quotes from the GT discussed in section 5 above, as the evidence
to support his claims. Unfortunately, Rotheim appears to have no
knowledge of mathematics. First, the "mathematical method" does
not assume strict independence of all factors nor does mathematics
make "everything a function of a single variable and assume that
all the partial differentials vanish" (Keynes, 1964, p. 275). Keynes
correctly calls such approaches "pseudo-mathematical" or places
the word mathematical in quotation marks. Keynes is attacking
the inappropriate and/or incorrect use of mathematics. Rotheim
appears to have assumed that Edgeworth's approach is synonymous
with, or representative of, the use of mathematics. Keynes knew
better, which is why he called Edgeworth's approach "quasi-

mathematical". The available textual comparison between Keynes' positive assessment of Ramsey's use of mathematics and negative assessment of Edgeworth's misuse of mathematics in Volume 10 of the CWJMK (1973), supports a rejection of Rotheim's position.

Rotheim's views, however, are only the latest in a series of such assessments. Carabelli claims that, in the GT, "Keynes referred to his analysis as logical and at the same time attacked the mathematical approach", (Carabelli, 1985, p. 166) or that "Keynes said that his approach in the 'General Theory', unlike the mathematical approach . . . was not a machine . . . which will furnish an infallible answer", (Carabelli, 1985, p. 153).

According to Skidelsky, "Keynes' attack on the Jevons/Edgeworth approach was in line with his general hostility to the use of mathematical methods in both probability and economics", (Skidelsky, 1983, p. 222). According to Rosenberg, Keynes "took part in a most unedifying exchange with the statistician Karl Pearson on the very possibility of quantitative social science. As Skidelsky notes, "had his criticism been accepted . . . practically all statistical investigation of social problems would have been ruled out of court", (Rosenberg, 1986, p. 12).

There is no support for any of these claims. All that Keynes can be accused of is preferring the more careful and circumspect use and assessment of mathematical methods made by Boole, DeMorgan, Poincare, Pierce, Ramsey and Marshall. What support is there for the assertion that the Jevons/Edgeworth approach is *the* only legitimate assessment of the proper role for mathematical analysis in social science? Keynes' attack is on the fanatical insistence on the part of Benthamite Utilitarians like Jevons, Edgeworth and Pearson, that single number "point estimates", based on the much less complete and lower quality data and information available in the social sciences, can be regarded as giving estimates that are as accurate and reliable as estimates obtained in hard science under strict laboratory controlled experimental conditions that are regularly replicated. Keynes' assessment of Pearson is no different from assessments like Gould's "The Mismeasure of Man" (1981), Kitcher's "Vaulting Ambition" (1985), Monagu's "Race and IQ"

(1975), or Lewontin, Rose and Kamin's "Not in our Genes" (1984). As far as I am aware, none of the above authors have been accused of being opposed to the use of mathematical and statistical methods in social science. However, they have certainly pointed out the very serious misuse of statistical and mathematical methods in educational psychology, sociobiology, genetics, criminology and heredity.

What is a reader to make of the following conjecture by Carabelli?

> "In the 'Treatise' the priority of ordinary language over mathematical language was unquestioned. 'I shall not cut myself [sic]', Keynes wrote, 'from the convenient' but looser, expressions which have been habitually employed by previous writers and have the advantage of being . . . immediately intelligible to the reader'. In the footnote, he praised ordinary language, in terms of its semantical character, contrasting it to the pure syntactical one of artificial mathematical language (Keynes, 1921, pp. 18-19). Just for its organic characteristics, its open structure and the non-finite number of propositions, its compatability with contradiction and its semantical character, ordinary language permitted one to deal with phenomena presenting [sic] the attribute of complexity". (Carabelli, 1985, p. 66). Carabelli does not change her view in her 1988 book).

In section 2 I covered both pages 18-19 and the footnote mentioned by Carabelli. There is no support for Carabelli's conjecture. Yet, all the reviews of her book, "On Keynes' Method", in the economic journals, characterize her assessment of Keynes as definitive (see Hamouda, 1990; Guthrie, 1989; or Dimand, 1989).

According to Rotheim, "Carabelli (1988) has persuasively characterized these two perspectives, which Keynes describes as "mathematical language" and "ordinary language", (Rotheim, p. 321). According to both Rotheim and Carabelli, Keynes rejected mathematical language and supported ordinary language. That this assessment has nothing to do with the points made by Keynes in the TP or GT can easily be checked by looking in the index of either book. No such categories or listing, even remotely related to such an issue, appear.

However, it may be that, in trying to make the following trivial point, a mountain has been made out of a mole hill. The point was made long ago by Ludwig Boltzmann, a mathematical physicist and statistician:

> His Lectures in theoretical physics were attended by many non-physicists, who could understand the problems which Boltzmann took care to state independently of the mathematical arguments. "The True Theoretician," he wrote, "makes only sparing use of formulae. It is in the books of the allegedly practical thinkers that one finds formulae only too frequently, and used for mere adornment." (Feyerbend, Paul, 1967, p. 334)

The point made by Boltzmann above is exactly what Keynes is saying on p. 275 and pp. 297-298 of the GT. However, to conclude that Keynes is rejecting mathematical analysis in favor of ordinary language is absurd, just as it would be absurd to conclude that Boltzmann favored ordinary language over mathematics. Each has an important role to play: Boltzmann and Keynes *both* used ordinary language *and* mathematics. There is no need to reject either language. Both are needed by the competent theorist.

7. Was Keynes mathematically incompetent?

J.K. Galbraith generally sums up the current, near unanimous, assessment of Keynes' analytic competence:

> "Keynes had long been suspect among his colleagues for the clarity of his writing and thought, the two often going together. In the General Theory, he redeemed his academic

reputation. It is a work of profound obscurity, badly written and prematurely published . . . Some of its influence derived from its being extensively incomprehensible. Other scholars were needed to construe its meaning, restate its propositions in intelligible form." (Galbraith, 1975, p. 218).

In particular, Lester Thurow states:

"The weakness of Keynesian analysis is that it does not have a micro-economic theory to defend its macro-economic assumptions in the other markets, such as the one for labor . . .," (Thurow, 1983, p. 7. See also p. 181).

These assessments are the conventional wisdom of practically all academic economists. Samuelson, Patinkin, Clower, Hicks, Klein, Robinson, and many others, have made similar assessments. Thus, Klant claims:

"Keynes refrained from formalizing his theories. In 'A Treatise on Money', he plays extensively with identities, and in 'The General Theory', he uses mathematics to make shorthand notes. Nowhere does he apply formal mathematical analysis", (Klant, 1985, p. 82).

The above mentioned economists are simply mistaken in their assessments. Keynes did formalize his "Theory of Effective Demand" in chapters 20, 21 and 10 of "The General Theory". His microeconomic foundations were that of the purely competitive firm-industry, combined with the marginal productivity theory of one variable input, labor. The footnotes in these chapters are not "shorthand notes", although they may appear to be so. What Keynes does is give his first step and his result, assuming that the reader is capable of filling in the details. Once these details are filled in, the reader will see Keynes' chapter 3 as the Boltzmann-like tour-de-force that it is (see Brady, 1990 and 1991 for the details).

Yet it was Keynes' own colleagues at Cambridge, Joan Robinson and Richard Kahn, who started the myth of Keynes, the mathematical illiterate:

> "I am reminded by a referee of Gerald Shove's remark, repeated by Keynes' contemporaries at Cambridge, that Maynard never took the twenty minutes necessary to learn the theory of value", (Leroy, 1983, p. 398, ft. 1).

Of course, it was Joan Robinson who claimed Shove made this statement *after* Shove had died. Keynes' exposition in chapters 20, 21 and 10 demonstrates this to be false. It would be interesting, from a history of thought perspective, to pinpoint exactly who else was involved. Whoever they were, they have led the economics profession into a quagmire and swamp of "Keynes interpretations" that have split the economics profession asunder.

8. Ramsey's misinterpretations of the TP

a.) Ramsey's misinterpretations in 1922

Let us start with the 1922 review. Ramsey claims:

> "First, he thinks that between any two non-self-contradictory propositions there holds a probability relation (Axiom I), for example between 'My carpet is blue' and 'Napoleon was a great general'; it is easily seen that it leads to contradictions to assign the probability 1 / 2 to such cases, and Mr Keynes would conclude that the probability is not numerical. But it would seem that in such cases there is no probability; that for a logical relation other than a truth function, to hold between two propositions, there must be some connection between them. If this be so, there is no such probability as the probability that 'my carpet is blue' given only that 'Napoleon was a great general', and there is

therefore no question of assigning a numerical value.
(Ramsey, 1989, p. 219-220)

Keynes' Axiom I (on p. 135 of the TP) requires his definition
on p. 4 of the TP, which requires "a logical connection between
one set of propositions (h) . . . and another set of propositions (a)"
(Keynes, 1921, pp. 5-6). Thus, "There is a *probability relation* of
degree alpha between a and h" (p. 4) That can be written as "a / h
= alpha" or as "a / h = P" or "a / h = P" (p. 40). Keynes states:

> "The value of the symbol a / h . . . lies in the fact that it
> contains explicit reference to the data to which the probability
> relates the conclusion". (Keynes, p. 40)

Ramsey's argument makes no sense, since there is no logical
connection or relation between the proposition "My carpet is blue"
and the proposition "Napoleon is a great general."

Second, Ramsey completely misinterprets Keynes' use of the
term "non-numerical". Now by "non-numerical" Keynes meant
not by a *single* numeral or number (see Keynes, 1921, p. 163).
Non-numerical probabilities require *two* numbers, a lower and an
upper bound or limit. Such non-numerical probabilities are called
interval estimates (Keynes, 1921, pp. 23, 24-28, 31, 32, 163,
237, 373-375) or indeterminate probabilities (p. 34). Non-
comparability (p. 34) simply means that the two intervals *overlap*.
If such *overlap* occurs, no comparison is possible in terms of more
or less. On p. 39, Keynes gives a graphical analysis. Probability A
is a probability measurable by a *single, unique* number. Probabilities
U, V, W, X, Y, Z are non numerical probabilities; that is they
require *two* numbers, a lower and upper bound. Probabilities are
numerically comparable only if they can be represented by a *single*
number. Thus, for Keynes, if $p_1 = .7$ and $p_2 = .8$, then $p_2 > p_1$. On
the other hand, if p_1 is *between* .6 and .8 while p_2 is *between* .7 and
.9, then p_1 and p_2 are *not comparable* using greater than or less
than symbols.

Ramsey claims that:

> "Mr Keynes is like a surveyor, who, afraid that his estimates of the heights of mountains might be erroneous, decided that were he to talk about actual heights he would be altogether adrift in the unknown; so he said that heights were relative to surveyors' instruments, and when he came to a mountain hidden in mist he assigned it a non-numerical height because he could not see if it were taller or shorter than the others. (Ramsey, 1922, p. 220)

Keynes' whole discussion in chapter 3 simply went over Ramsey's head. Further, Ramsey never got around to ever reading chapter 15 and 17 of the TP where Keynes operationalized his interval estimate approach first suggested by Keynes in chapter 5 of the TP. Ramsey next attacks Keynes' Principle of Indifference in claiming that:

> "The true solution of the difficulty seems to depend on Mr Johnson's notion 'The Determinable'. The Principle of Indifference may be stated as follows: Relative to evidence, on which it is certain, that a given subject has one other of a finite number of absolute determinates under the same determinable, the probabilities that the subject has each of those absolute determinates are equal, provided that the evidence is symmetrical with regard to the various alternatives. (Ramsey, 1922, p. 221)

Ramsey totally ignores Keynes' discussion on pp.60-63 of the TP which is IDENTICAL to Johnson's supposedly superior formulation.

Next, Ramsey claims that:

> "In Part II, Mr. Keynes gives a symbolic deduction of the formulae of the calculus of probabilities from definitions

and axioms; this has a minor flaw. Mr. Keynes conceals two important axioms in definitions; defining the *sum* of *ab/h, a ~ b/h* as *a/h* and the *product* of *a/bh, b/h* as *ab/h*, he conceals the assumptions that the sum and product so defined are always unique, *i.e.,* that if *ab/h = cd/k,* (= P), *a ~ b/h = c ~ d/ k,* (= Q) then *a/h = c/k,* (= PQ); and that if *a/bh = c/dk,* (= P), *b/h = d/k,* (= Q) then *ab/h = cd/k,* (= PQ). (Ramsey, p. 221)

Contrary to Ramsey, there is no minor flaw and no axioms are being concealed in definitions.

Keynes attempted to provide an axiomatic foundation for *both* numerical *and* non-numerical probabilities. He gave separate axiomatic foundations to frequencies (chapter 8) and numerical probabilities. (Chapter 15)

Thus,

> "If we were to assume that probabilities or ratios . . . But in the absence of such an assumption, it is necessary to give a meaning by definition to those processes (of addition and multiplication).
>
> Thus, we have to introduce as definitions what would be axioms if the meaning of addition and multiplication were already defined." (Keynes, 1921 pp. 133-136)

Finally,

> "A meaning has not been given . . . to the signs of addition and multiplication between probabilities *in all cases.*" (Keynes, 1921, p. 137).

In fact, "sums and products do no exist between every pair of probabilities," (Keynes, p. 138). Keynes' analysis simply went over Ramsey's head.

Ramsey's last criticism concerns Keynes' definition of random.

> "Lastly we may note that Mr. Keynes' definition of 'random' suggests that he may be wrong in his fundamental

conception of probability. For in it occurs the probability phi*(x)/S(x)* · *h;* and it is considered whether this is equal to phi*(x)/S(x)* · *h* · *x* = *a* = Phi*(a)/S(a)* · *h.*" (Ramsey, p. 222)

Of course, Keynes' discussions on pp 291-292 and 412-416 relate to his special frequency theory of probability which is a *special* case of his logical approach when Keynes' early version of sensitivity or robustness analysis (Lexis' Q statistic involving the *stability* of the frequency series) shows that the different sub series are all convergent to the series frequency. Contrary to Ramsey there is not "a new kind of probability." (Ramsey, p. 222).

b.) Ramsey's Misinterpretations in 1926

At this point, the reader may ask, "How did Ramsey's 1922 review get published?" We now proceed to the 1926 review. Unfortunately, Ramsey does no better. In fact, he does a lot worse even though he supposedly had an additional four plus years to read and digest the TP.
Ramsey claims that:

> "I think it is a pity that Mr. Keynes did not see this clearly, because the exactitude of this correspondence would have provided quite as worthy material for his scepticism as did the numerical measurement of probability relations. Indeed some of his arguments against their numerical measurement appear to apply quite equally well against their exact correspondence with degrees of belief; for instance, he argues that if rates of insurance correspond to subjective, i.e. actual, degrees of belief, these are not rationally determined, and we cannot infer that probability relations can be similarly measured. It might be argued that the true conclusion in such a case was not that, as Mr. Keynes thinks, to the non-numerical probability relation corresponds a non-numerical degree of rational belief, but that degrees of belief, which were always numerical, did not correspond one to one with the probability relations justifying them." (Ramsey, 1926, p. 22)

Ramsey again repeats his gross misunderstanding and misinterpretation of Keynes' term "non-numerical." See my discussion above.

Ramsey then claims:

> "But let us now return to a more fundamental criticism of Mr. Keynes' views, which is the obvious one that there really do not seem to be any such things as the probability relations he describes." (Ramsey, 1926, p. 22)

and

> "If, on the other hand, we take the simplest possible pairs of propositions such as 'This is red' and 'That is blue' or 'This is red' and 'That is red' whose logical relations should surely be easiest to see, no one, I think, pretends to be sure what is the probability relation which connects them." (Ramsey, 1926 p. 23)

Of course, Keynes' degree of partial belief involves a logical connection. Thus,

> "Probability is, so for as measurement is concerned, closely analogues to similarity." (Keynes, 1921, p. 28)

and

> "But the closest analogy is that of similarity . . . There are also, as in the case of probability, *different* orders of similarity." (Keynes, p. 36)

Ramsey's example of "This is red" and "That is blue" or "This is red" and "That is red" above is, in fact, a deliberate misinterpretation of Keynes' example on p. 36 of the TP:

> "For instance a book bound in blue morocco is more like a book bound in red morocco than if it were bound in

blue calf; and a book bound in red calf is more like the book in red morocco then if it were in blue calf. But there may be no comparison between the degree of similarity which exists between books bound in red morocco and blue morocco, and that which exists between books bound in red morocco and red calf. This illustration deserves special attention, as the analogy between orders of similarity and probability is so great that its apprehension will greatly assist that of the ideas I wish to convey. We say that one argument is more probable than another . . . in the same kind of way as we can describe one object as more like than another to a standard object of comparison." (Keynes, p. 36).

Ramsey's argument is that is unable to see any degree of similarity between different colors. This means that Ramsey does not understand argument from analogy. In this area of thought, Ramsey's thought processes are sadly deficient as can be seen by the logical mess Ramsey proceeds to create throughout section 2 of his paper.

Unable to comprehend the concept of degree of similarity (analogy), Ramsey falls deeper and deeper into his intellectual quagmire.

> "We shall, I think, find that this view of the calculus of probability removes various difficulties that have hitherto been found perplexing. In the first place it gives us a clear justification for the axioms of the calculus, which on such a system as Mr. Keynes' is entirely wanting. For now it is easily seen that if partial beliefs are consistent, they will obey these axioms, but it is utterly obscure why Mr. Keynes' mysterious logical relations should obey them[7]. We should be so curiously ignorant of the instances of these relations, and so curiously knowledgeable about their general laws. (Ramsey, 1926, p. 40)

First, Keynes' comparative degree of partial connection or logical connection or similarity or analogy or partial belief or partial symmetry or relative partial belief or relative partial relation is not mysterious, except to Ramsey. Second, in his footnote 6, Ramsey repeats the same errors about Keynes' definitions and axioms of addition and multiplication that he first presented in his 1922 review.

Ramsey next claims that:

> "Secondly, the Principle of Indifference can now be altogether dispensed with; we do not regard it as belonging to formal logic to say what should be a man's expectation of drawing a white or a black ball from an urn; his original expectations may within the limits of consistency be any he likes; all we have to point out is that if he has certain expectations he is bound in consistency to have certain others." (Ramsey, p. 40)

Hans-Werner Sinn, in the May, 1981 issue of the Quarterly Journal of Economics, proved Ramsey's argument to be false. The reader is directed to that article for Sinn's extensive demonstration that Ramsey's subjectivist approach rests on a camouflaged or disguised resort to the POI. Finally, Ramsey claims that:

> "But anyone who tries to decide by Mr. Keynes' methods what are the proper alternatives to regard as equally probable in molecular mechanics, e.g. in Gibbs' phase-space, will soon be convinced that it is a matter of physics rather than pure logic. (Ramsey, p. 40)

Contrary to Ramsey, Keynes never claimed otherwise. In fact it is a mere semantic game to claim that one is not using the principle of indifference apriori, but simply making a "special" hypothesis in each care about the initial distributions of gas particles. An application of the principle of indifference (POI) to the classical theory of Boltzman gives a probability of 1/9 for each distribution. An application of the POI to the theory of Bose-Einstein gives a probability for each distribution of 1/6. An application to the theory of Dirac-Fermi, using another "special" hypothesis, would give an answer for each distribution of 1/3. An application of POI gives the *exact same* answer in each case. Why Ramsey dismisses "Keynes' method" without providing the reader with the fact that Keynes' *answers* are IDENTICAL to the answers arrived at by any competent physicist is the real mystery.

c.) The Assessment of Ramsey's reviews-Pro

I will give two assessments which are favorable to Ramsey. R. Monk claims that:

> "His first published work dates from when he was 19. In 1922, he published three short pieces. A devastation critique of Keynes' theory of probability . . ." (Monk, BRS News, #72, 1991, p. 26).

D.H. Mellor claims that:

> "But it did not satisfy Ramsey, whose objections to it— some of them published before he was nineteen—were so cogent and comprehensive that Keynes himself abandoned it." (Mellor, 1995, p. 247).

These conclusions are quite astounding. There is nothing devastating in these reviews, concerning Keynes' work, except Ramsey's ignorance. Ramsey's comments are not cogent and comprehensive, but silly and based primarily on chapter 1-4 of the TP.

d.) The Assessment of Ramsey's Reviews-Con

> ". . . those who claim to perceive a probability relation which others do not perceive are naturally heard with scepticism, although it may well be that they are in the right. Ramsey argues that Mr. Keynes does not himself

perceive this relation, but a negative of this sort is always difficult to establish." (Russell, 1931. In Russell, 1996, p. 111)

Continuing,

"Ramsey's theory of probability is, to my mind, less penetrating than his work on mathematical logic . . . Probability, if concerned with degrees of belief, is concerned with what they ought to be, not with what they in fact are. What they ought to be must depend on something objective which ought therefore to be used as the definition of probability." (Russell, 1931. In Russell, 1996, pp. 111-112)

In 1932, Russell stated that Ramsey's essay "is . . . less valuable then most of the other essays." (Russell, 1996, p. 117) In 1959, Russell published his final comments on the issue of the logic of probability in chapter 16 of his *My Philosophical Development*, titled "Non-Demonstrative Inference." Russell's support for Keynes' approach is overwhelmingly supported. The criticism of Ramsey (and Karl Popper) are not ever alluded to, although Russell does discuss or mention much of Ramsey's other work.

e.) Conclusion

In neither of Ramsey's two reviews is *any* compelling or clear cut argument laid out, in a coherent, comprehensive fashion, that would lead a competent logician to reject Keynes' approach in the TP. It should be noted that for Ramsey, a decision is a function of *only* one variable, its probability (subjective) multiplied by the utility of the outcome. There is absolutely no role, in Ramsey's system, for Keynes' weight of the evidence (argument) variable, w, which serves as a measure of the degree of confidence a decision maker has in the probabilities. This is due to the fact that Ramsey mistakenly assumes that probabilities *are* measures of the degree of confidence. Ramsey thus conflates "degree of belief" with "degree of confidence". The "Ellsberg Paradox Literature," Allais Paradox Literature and preference reversal literature, which now lists thousands of articles and hundreds of books, all directly supports Keynes' weight of the evidence criteria while calling into question Ramsey's deficient argument.

9. Conclusion

J.M. Keynes received his undergraduate degree in mathematics. He made extensive use of mathematical technique in both the TP and GT. However, like Boltzmann, he attempted to put his analysis in a form that would allow the largest number of practicing economists to follow his argument verbally, independent of the mathematical framework.

The argument that Keynes was opposed to the use of legitimate mathematical analysis is unsupported, as is the charge that Keynes was analytically incompetent.

Finally, the claim, that for Keynes, probabilities were primarily non-numerical, is the result of a serious semantical misinterpretation or a failure to read the relevant chapters in the TP. Keynes was an ordinalist, who believed that cardinal measurement was generally not attainable. Thus, a ranking of alternatives, ordinal measurement, was the appropriate tool to use. Such a ranking approach complemented Keynes' inexact "interval estimate" approach.

Footnotes

[1]   For instance, see Samuelson, 1946, pp. 191, 193, 198; Galbraith, 1975, pp. 217-218; Klein, 1946, pp. 81-83; Patinkin, 1976, pp. 22-23, 92; 1979, p. 159; 1982, pp. 144-158; 1989, pp. 537-538; Robinson, 1964, p. ix; or Stone (1978).

[2]   See Leroy, 1983, p. 398, ft. 1.

[3]   See Savage, 1981.

[4]   See Gleick, J. 1987, pp. 92-93, 123, 321, 181-82, 250-252, 257-58.

[5]   See Appenix I.

[6]   See Stone, 1978; Klein, 1951 or Klant, 1985.

[7]   It appears in Mr. Keynes' system as if the principal axioms—the laws of
       addition and multiplication—were nothing but definitions. This is merely
       a logical mistake; his definitions are formally invalid unless corresponding
       axioms are presupposed. Thus his definition of multiplication presupposes
       the law that if the probability of a given bh is equal to that of c given dk,
       and the probability of b given h is equal to that of d given k, then will the
       probabilities of ab given h and of cd given k be equal.

References

Bateman, Bradley. 1987. "Keynes' Changing Conception of
      Probability." Economics and Philosophy 3:97-119.

Boole, George. 1952. Collected Logical Works. The Laws of
      Thought (1854). Vol. II. LaSalle, Illinois: Open Court
      Publishing Company.

Brady, Michael E. 1983. The Foundation of Keynes' Macrotheory:
      His Logical Theory of Probability and Its Application in The
      General Theory and After. Unpublished dissertation, UC
      Riverside, California.

Brady, Michael E. 1987. "J.M. Keynes' Theory of Evidential
      Weight: Its Relation to Information Processing Theory and
      Application in The General Theory." Synthese 71:37-59.

Brady, Michael E. 1988. "J.M. Keynes' Position on The General
      Applicability of Mathematical, Logical and Statistical Methods
      in Economics and Social Science." Synthese 76:1-24.

Brady, Michael E. 1990. "The Mathematical Development of
      Keynes' Aggregate Supply Function in The General Theory."
      History of Political Economy 22:167-172.

Brady, Michael E. 1989. "A Restatement of Keynes' Theory of
      Effective Demand based on The Microeconomic Analysis in
      Chapter 20 of The General Theory".

Carabelli, Anna. 1988. "Keynes on Cause, Chance, and Possibility."
      In Lawson and Pesaron (eds.), Keynes' Economics
      Methodological Issues. New York:ME Sharpe:151-180.

Carabelli, Anna. 1988. On Keynes' Method. New York, St. Martins Press.

Dimand, R.W. 1989. Book Review. Economic Journal, 99:890-891.

Favereau, Oliver. 1988. "Probability and Uncertainty: After All Keynes Was Right".

Economia, serie. . PE de La Revue Economies et Societes, 133-167.

Galbraith, J.K. 1975. Money. Boston:Houghton Mifflin.

Garner, C. Alan. 1983. "Comment." History of Political Economy 15:83-86.

Gleick, James. 1987. CHAOS. New York:Penguin Books.

Gould, Stephen J. 1981. The Mismeasure of Man. New York. W.W. Norton.

Guthrie, William. 1989. Book Review. Southern Economic Journal.

Hamouda, O.F. 1990. Book Review. Journal of Economic Literature 28:79-80.

Keynes, J.M. 1921. A Treatise on Probability. London: Macmillan.

Keynes, J.M. 1937. "The General Theory of Employment". Quarterly Journal of Economics 51:209-223.

Keynes, J.M. 1964. The General Theory of Employment, Interest and Money, New York:Harcourt, Brace and World.

Keynes, J.M. 1972. Essays in Biography. Vol. X, The Collected Writings of John Maynard Keynes (CWJMK), D. Maggridge (ed.). London: Macmillan.

Kitcher, Philip. 1985. Vaulting Ambition: Sociobiology and the Quest for Human Nature. Massachusetts: Massachusetts Institute of Technology Press.

Klant, J.J. 1985. 'The Slippery Transition." In Lawson an Pesaran, op. cit., pp. 80-98.

Klein, Lawrence. 1946. The Keynesian Revolution. New York: Macmillan.

Klein, Lawrence. 1951. "The Life of John Maynard Keynes." Journal of Political Economy 59:

Lawson, Tony. 1985. "Uncertainty and Economic Analysis." Economic Journal 95:909-927.

Lawson, Tony. 1987. "The Relative/Absolute Nature of Knowledge and Economic Analysis." Economic Journal 97:951-970.

Lawson, Tony. 1988. "Probability and Uncertainty in Economic Analysis." Journal of Post Keynesian Economics 11:38-65.

Leroy, Stephen F. 1983. "Keynes' Theory of Investment." History of Political Economy 15:397-421.

Lewontin, R.C., S. Rose and L. Kamin. 1984. Not in Our Genes. New York. Random House.

Mellor, D.H. 1995. "E.P. Ramsey", Philosophy, 70, pp. 243-257.

Monk, R. 1991. "Russell and Ramsey", London Reviews of Books, 29 August, pp. 11-13. Reprinted in Russell Society News, No. 72, (Nov., 1991) pp. 25-26.

Montagu, Ashley (ed.). 1975. Race and IQ. Oxford. Oxford University Press.

Patinkin, Don. 1976. Keynes' Monetary Thought. Durham: Duke University Press.

Patinkin, Don. 1978. "Keynes' Aggregate Supply Function." History of Political Economy 10:577-596.

Patinkin, Don. 1979. "A Study of Keynes' Theory of Effective Demand." Economic Inquiry 17:155-176.

Patinkin, Don. 1980. "New Materials on the Development of Keynes' Monetary Thought." History of Political Economy 12:1-29.

Patinkin, Don. 1982. Anticipation of the General Theory? and Other Essays on Keynes. Chicago. University of Chicago Press.

Patinkin, Don. 1989. "Keynes and the Keynesian Cross: A Further Note." History of Political Economy 21:537-544.

Ramsey, Frank P. 1922. "Mr. Keynes on Probability" The Cambridge Magazine, Vol. XI, 3-5. Reprinted in BJ PS, 1989, 40, 219-222.

Ramsey, Frank P. 1928. "A Mathematical Theory of Savings." Economic Journal 38:543-559.

Ramsey, Frank P. 1926. "Truth and Probability." The Foundations of Mathematics, ed. by R.B. Braithwaite. London: Routledge and Kegan Paul. pp. 156-198 Also in Foundations of Bayesian Decision Theory, pp. 19-47.

Robinson, Joan. 1964. Economic Heresies. Cambridge. Cambridge University Press.

Rosenberg, Alexander. 1986. Book Review. Los Angeles Times Book Review, 4-27-1986. p. 12.

Rotheim, Roy J. 1988. "Keynes and the Language of Probability and Uncertainty." Journal of Post Keynesian Economics 11:82-100.

Rotheim, Roy J. 1989-90. "Organicism and the Role of the Individual in Keynes' Thought." Journal of Post Keynesian Economics 12:316-326.

Russell, B. 1930. "Probability and Fact", Atlantic Monthly 146, pp. 163-170.

Russell, B. 1931. "Review of Ramsey", Mind, 40, pp. 476-482. Reprinted in Russell, 1996.

Russell, B. 1932. "Review of Ramsey", Philosophy, 7, pp. 84-86. Reprinted in Russell, 1996.

Russell, B. 1959. My Philosophical Development. Unwin Book: London.

Russell, B. 1996. Collected Papers of Bertrand Russell. Volio, Edited by J.G. Slater and P. Köllner. Routledge: London.

Samuelson, Paul. 1946. "Lord Keynes and The General Theory." Econometrica 14:187-200.

Savage, L.J. 1971. "Elicitation of Personal Probabilities and Expectations." In The Writings of Leonard Jimmie Savage. American Statistical Association and Institute of Mathematical Statistics, 1981. Washington, D.C. pp. 565-614.

Sinn, H-W. 1980. "A Rehabilitation of The Principle of Insufficient Reason", Quarterly Journal of Economics, 75, 493-506.

Skidelsky, Robert, 1983. John Maynard Keynes: Hopes Betrayed (1883-1920). Vol. I. London: MacMillan.

Stohs, Mark. 1980. "'Uncertainty' in Keynes' General Theory." History of Political Economy 12:372-382.

Stohs, Mark. 1983. "Rejoinder." History of Political Economy 15:87-91.

Stone, Richard. 1978. Keynes, Political Arithmetic and Econometrics. The British Academy, London, England.

Thurow, Lester C. 1983. Dangerous Currents. The State of Economics. New York. New York. Random House.

Appendix I

The failure to read the TP has led to strange results. Several such examples in the literature are covered in this appendix. For Keynes, most probabilities were "non-numerical". However, by numerical Keynes meant the assignment of a single number to represent a probability. Thus, by non-numerical, Keynes meant that a single cardinal number could rarely represent the probability relation. In other words, "exact" or "precise" or "definite" numerical calculation was limited. However, in its place he put ordinal rankings or comparisons, or, what he called "inexact" numerical comparison, using upper and lower limits or bounds, i.e. intervals. In particular, he showed how Boole's system could be adapted for "inexact numerical approximation", establishing l. u. b's and g. 1. b's. Yet, the failure of economists to either read chapter 5 or Part II of the TP, has lead to a deadend conclusion, that Keynes' method, whatever it was, was non-operational:

> "If we admit, then, that Keynes still allows that some type of probability calculation can be made, what type is it? And further, what type of 'scientific' calculation cannot be made?", (Stohs, 1980, p. 379).
>
> "One problem is that Keynes does not specify in the General Theory how we are to carry out the probability calculations . . . We can assume, at least, that these would be non-numerical calculations", (Stohs, 1980, p. 380).
>
> "However, what did Keynes mean by the word 'calculable'? It seems clear that he ruled out numerical probability calculations, but what about Stohs' 'non-numerical calculations'? Indeed, what is a non-numerical probability calculation?", (Garner, 1983, p. 84).
>
> "Garner also asks for an explanation of this non-numerical notion of probability. Keynes never fully explained this notion . . .," (Stohs, 1983, p. 90, ft. 15).

The reader should note the close correspondence of Stohs-Garnert to Ramsey on this point.

From their article footnotes, it appears that Stohs and Garner read no more of the TP than chapters 1-3 and chapter 6. Thus, on this particular point, the Stohs-Garner exchange has seriously led the economics profession astray. That Keynes had some as yet unfathomable, mysterious, non-numerical concept, has been accepted as fact in the literature. Thus, Lawson asserts ". . . in Keynes' account uncertainty is associated with a situation wherin numerically determinate probabilities are not to be had," (Lawson, 1988, p. 46). "Uncertainty corresponds to a situation in which probabilities are not numerically determinate . . .", (Lawson, 1988, p. 48). Thus, according to Lawson, economists should "follow" Keynes ". . . in regarding uncertainty as corresponding to situations wherin numerically measureable probabilistic knowledge is not available," (Lawson, 1988, p. 62. See also Lawson, 1985, p. 914 and 1987, p. 955 for nearly identical statements).

Of course, Keynes *never* held the views foisted upon him by Stohs, Garner and Lawson. Keynes' view was that

> "The results of our endeavors are very uncertain, but we have a genuine probability, even when the evidence upon which it is founded is slight," (Keynes, 1921, p. 310).

However, the genuine probability Keynes is talking about is a "non-numerical" interval estimate and not a "numerical" point estimate. It is this confusion about "non-numerical" that has led to an assessment of Keynes' views on probability that are totally at odds with his TP analysis. The original source of this confusion can be traced to F.P. Ramsey's claim that Keynes had some kind of strange mysterious logical relation that *required* non-numerical comparison. Bertrand Russell is certainly correct about his assessment of Ramsey's work when he pointed out that Ramsey's essay on probability had the *least* value compared to any of the other essays.

2

The Meaning Of Probability And Uncertainty In Keynes' Treatise On Probability And The General Theory A Refutation Of Stohs, Garner, And Ramsey

1. Introduction

Hugh Townsend, in a letter to Keynes of November 25, 1938, was the first economist to clearly comprehend the close correspondence between Keynes' Treatise on Probability, hereafter designated as (TP), and the General Theory, hereafter designed as (GT).[1]

> "This is the nearest I can get to an analysis of the part played by the factor of confidence in the rationale of interest. I believe that its further logical analysis at a deeper level of generalization is connected with the part played by the weight of evidence in your Theory of Probability, but I cannot see just how."

Keynes[2] replied that,

> ". . . There is very little in that letter from which I want to differ . . . As regards my remarks in my General Theory, have you taken account of what I say at page 240, as well as

what I say at page 148, which is the passage I think you previously quoted? I am rather inclined to associate risk premium with probability, strictly speaking, and liquidity premium with what in my Treatise on Probability I called weight."

On page 240 of the GT, Keynes admits that in earlier chapters he did not discuss how to estimate either the risk premium or the liquidity premium. He then again refers the reader to the footnote on page 148 of the GT. In this footnote, Keynes links "very uncertain" to his concept of weight. However, Chapter Six of the TP contains only the logical formulation of the concept of weight, based on the concept of a logic of relevance developed earlier in Chapters 4 and 5 and later extended in section 3 of Chapter 14.[3] However, on page 83, footnote 1 of the TP, Keynes directs the reader to Chapter 26. It is in Chapter 26 that Keynes gives the estimation (comparison) procedures for the risk and liquidity premiums.[4]

The conclusion to be drawn is that what Keynes meant by "uncertainty" or "very uncertain" in the TP is identical to what he meant in the GT. Keynes' concept of weight, developed first logically in Chapter Six and then quantitatively in Chapter 26 of the TP, is the basic foundation for Keynes' liquidity preference theory. Weight (uncertainty) is the foundation for his theory of interest. Further, Keynes' concepts of risk and probability are likewise the same for both the TP and the GT.

2. The Stohs-Garner Argument

Stohs states:

"The first consideration is that the terms 'uncertain' and 'improbable' are used interchangeably in Keynes' Treatise on Probability. Yet, we have seen that Keynes states in the General Theory that 'very uncertain' does not have the same meaning as 'very improbable'. The solution resides in another

passage in the Treatise on Probability in which he mentions
another use of the term 'uncertain':

     'It must be added that the term 'certainty' is sometimes
used in a merely psychological sense to describe a state of
mind without reference to the logical grounds of the
belief. With this sense I am not concerned'. (Keynes,
1921, p. 16.).

     The inference to be made on the basis of this passage
would be that Keynes is using this psychological sense of
the term 'uncertainty' in his General Theory."[5]

    First, the terms "uncertain" and "improbable" are not used
interchangeably in the TP. In fact, the term "improbable" is
used only 23 times by Keynes on 20 pages of the TP.[6] Keynes
only mentioned the term "uncertain" or "uncertainty" a total
of 10 times on 9 pages of the TP.[7] The quote given by Stohs is
a preliminary to Keynes' attempt to provide a consistent, strict
set of definitions. "Certainty" (maximum probability) is equal
to one. Impossibility is equal to zero. Between 0 and 1 there
exist probable non-homogeneous "degrees of certainty". Neither
"uncertain" nor "improbable" is defined formally in Part II. The
use of these imprecise terms could only serve to confuse the reader[8]
of the TP.

    Stohs' quote of Keynes does not make much sense if it is
supposed to relate to "uncertainty", as the quote deals only with
"certainty", not "uncertainty".

    Second, Keynes is not using the term "uncertainty" in the
psychological sense of the term. All of the uses of "uncertain" or
"uncertainty", except on page 5 of the TP, refer to a lack of weight,
evidence, knowledge or information. This can be seen most clearly
by a reading of Chapter 26 of the TP. It is here that Keynes uses
the term, "very uncertain", for the only time in the TP. The meaning
of "very uncertain" is definitely tied to a lack of weight. It is a
logical relation, independent of a probability concept, that was
developed in Chapter Six and applied in Chapter 26, as the title of
that chapter, Applications of Probability to Conduct, implies.

Keynes states:

> "The results of our endeavors are very uncertain, but we have a genuine probability even when the evidence upon which it is founded is slight . . ."

Keynes then goes on to quote a nearly identical phrase used by Bishop Butler, an early empiricist logician where "greatly uncertain" stands in for "very uncertain". Keynes[10] further emphasizes the definitional equivalence between weight and uncertainty:

> "In chapter six, of Part I, the significance of 'weight' has been discussed. In the present connection, the question comes to this—if two probabilities are equal in degree, ought we, in choosing our course of action, to prefer that one which is based on a greater body of knowledge? . . . the degree of completeness of the information . . . does seem to be relevant, as well as the actual magnitude of the probability, in making practical decisions . . .
>
> 8. The last difficulty concerns the question, whether, the former difficulties being waived, the 'mathematical expectation' of different courses of action accurately measures what our preferences ought to be—whether . . . the undesirability of a given course of action increases in direction proportion to any increase in the uncertainty of its attaining its object or whether some allowance ought to be made for 'risk', its undesirability increasing more than in proportion to its uncertainty."

Keynes next develops a quantitative measure allowing one to compare different outcomes. He defines A as the outcome, p as the probability, where $p+q=1$ and E as the mathematical expectation. Risk is defined as $R=qE$. The conventional co-efficient of weight and risk is defined as $c=2pw/[(1+q)(1+w)]$, or as $p[2w/(1+w)][1/(1+q)]$. c is a continuous, non-linear convex function of p and w.

The non-linearity is caused by the [2w/(1+w)] factor as well as 1/(1+q). This is illustrated graphically below.

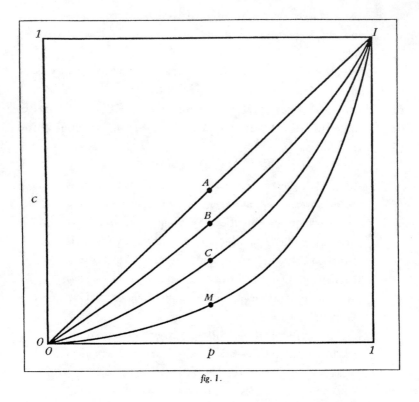

fig. 1.

Let OAI represent the numerical probability relation between 0 and 1 with weight, w, =1. Curve OCI represents non-numerical cases with o<w<1. A curve where w< the w of OCI is ODI. A curve with a w> the w of OCI is OBI. Thus as w increases, c approaches closer and closer to OAI. Since there is never any possibility of ever having too much evidence, except in games of chance where w=1, since the sample space never changes, the line OAI represents an ideal, platonic goal which can be approached but never attained in the real world. Applications of Keynes c co-efficient of risk and weight are in general agreement with the empirical fact that probabilities in real life are usually under weighted by about 10-

15 percent. This under weighting is due to the fact that real world decision makers realize that they rarely, if ever, have a complete information set.[11] [12]

In his reply to Garner, Stohs[13] still maintains the same position of his earlier contribution. Garner[14], in his comment, agrees with Stohs on this point.

The second point that needs to be made concerns both Stohs' and Garner's frequent queries concerning how ". . . we are to carry out the probability calculations of prospective yields. We can assume, at least, that this would be non-numerical calculation."[15]

Now Keynes was very clear at a number of points throughout his Treatise. Keynes' non-numerical logical relation is *no* different from the non-numerical notion of ordinal utility theory, i.e. an ordinal, comparative ranking. As in utility theory, no cardinal number needs to be calculated in order for a consumer to make a quantitative decision.

However, it is very important to recognize that Keynes distinguishes *exact* from *inexact* numerical calculation. While exact or precise numerical calculation *is* a strictly limited class requiring his principle of indifference in order to assign probabilities symmetrically, inexact numerical calculations, using upper and lower limits or intervals, forms a much larger class. Keynes[16] introduces his inexact approach in Chapter 5 of the TP, first laying out the logical foundation with his relevance relation.

> "In chapter 15, I bring the non-numerical theory of probability developed in the preceding chapters into connection with the usual numerical conception of it, and demonstrate how and on what class of cases a meaning can be given to a numerical measure of a relation of probability. This leads us to what may be termed numerical approximation . . . the relating of probabilities, which are not themselves numerical, by means of greater and less, by which in some cases numerical limits may be ascribed to probabilities which are not capable of numerical measure."

In Chapter 15, Keynes[17] goes to great detail in applying Boole's method by using upper-lower limits or bounds. Thus,

> "The sphere of inexact numerical comparison is not, however, quite so limited. Many probabilities, which are incapable of numerical measurement, can be placed, nevertheless between numerical limits. And by taking particular non-numerical probabilities as standards a great number of comparisons or approximate measurements become possible. If we can place a probability in an order of magnitude with some standard probability, we can obtain its approximate measure by comparison."

Keynes then proceeds to give a clear example using Charles Darwin. The rest of the chapter concerns Keynes' adapting work done by Boole into a method for the inexact calculation of approximate measures.[18]

3. Ramsey's Misinterpretation and Connection to the Stohs—Garner Exchange

Although neither Stohs or Garner realize it, their basic argument about Keynes' mysterious non-numerical calculations is identical to one of Ramsey's two major objections to Keynes' approach, which was that Keynes supposedly argued, ". . . that to the non-numerical probability relation corresponds a non-numerical degree of rational belief . . ." (Ramsey, 1926, p. 72), and that Keynes' axioms of addition and multiplication are in conflict with the "utterly obscure . . . mysterious logical relations" of "Mr. Keynes" (Ramsey, 1926, p. 40).

Of course, Keynes' argument throughout the TP is that probabilities can't be measured *by a single number or numeral*. It takes *two* numbers to measure a probability value in general. Thus, "non-numerical" does not mean that there is "a non-numerical height" (Ramsey, 1972, p. 220) or non-numerical weight, etc. This type of misrepresentation by Ramsey is just silly. What Keynes is arguing for is the use of interval estimates. A decision maker can thus calculate an upper bound and a lower bound. If he knows the particular *form* of the probability distribution (say, normal or binomial) then this interval will be small. If he does not know the precise type of distribution to apply, the interval (using Chebyshev's Inequality) will be quite large.

4. Keynes, Non-Comparability and Multiattributes

In Chapter 3 of the TP, Keynes pointed out that some probabilities may not be comparable using greater than or less than relations. An example will demonstrate Keynes' point. Suppose we wish to compare two interval estimates. The first interval is that the probability, p_1, lies somewhere between .5 and .6, or [.5, .6]. Suppose p_2 is estimated to be somewhere between .45 and .55, or [.45, .55]. Is $p_1=p_2$, $p_1>p_2$, or $p_1<p_2$? In fact, the answer is none of the above.

Keynes' second point was that a particular object of analysis, i.e., a book, has different attributes. Suppose we consider *size* and *color*, i.e., the probability of the book being "large" is equal to .75 while the probability of the book being red is .70. The probabilities are not comparable *in a logical sense* because there is no similarity or connection between the color of an object and the size of an object (or the *weight* of an object or the *age* of an object, etc.).

5. Conclusions

Keynes, very clearly but also very succinctly, on page 240 of the General Theory, directed the reader to Chapter Six of the TP. An obvious question is why not directly direct the reader to Chapter 26 of the TP. The answer is that logical foundation of relevance and weight had to be developed and understood first in Chapter Six of the TP (also probably Chapters 4 and 5), in order for the reader to be able to grasp the quantitative development of weight in Chapter 26 of the TP.

The first economist to see some connection was Hugh Townsend. Since he was the first, he should receive the credit for recognizing the close connection between Keynes' concept of weight in the TP and the equivalent concept of uncertainty in the GT, which served as the underpinning for Keynes' theories of the rate of interest, liquidity preference, and money. Unfortunately, the original paper Townsend sent Keynes was lost.

The Stohs-Garner characterization of Keynes' logical probability calculus as "non-numerical" represents an error of interpretation equivalent to the original error introduced into the literature by F.P. Ramsey in 1922 and 1926. Contrary to both Ramsey and Stohs-Garner, by "non-numerical" Keynes simply meant *not by a single numeral*. Instead, Keynes emphasized the use of indeterminate probabilities that required *two* numerals to estimate the probability value, i.e., *interval estimates*.

Unfortunately, this severe misrepresentation of Keynes' conceptual approach even finds expression in the article by D. Stove that appears in the Encyclopedia of Philosophy. Stove, in an otherwise excellent piece, states:

> "There are two negative Theses which distinguish Keynes' philosophy of probability from most earlier or later formulations. One is that probabilities simply do not have a numerical value . . . and never in normal inductive contexts. The other is that there are noncomparable probabilities . . . that are neither equal to nor greater nor less than one another. For obvious reasons, these theses have contributed to the neglect of Keynes by statistical writers" (Stove, 1967, p. 333).

This is simply wrong.

References

Gardenfors, P. 1978. "The Logic of Relevance". Syntheses 38: 351-68.

Garner, C. Alan. 1983. "'Uncertainty' in Keynes' General Theory: a comment". History of Political Economy 15: 83-86.

Keynes, J.M. 1973. A Treatise on Probability. In the Collected Writings of John Maynard Keynes (CWJMK).

_____. 1964. The General Theory of Employment Interest and Money. New York: Harcourt, Brace and World.

Moggridge, D. (ed.). 1979. Collected Works of J.M. Keynes. Vol. 29. London: MacMillan-Cambridge University Press, Vol. 29.

Ramsey, F.P. (1922). "Mr. Keynes on Probability". Cambridge Magazine, Vol. XI, 3-5. Reprinted in *BJPS*, 1989, 40, 219-222.

Ramsey, F.P. (1926). "Truth and Probability". *In the Foundations of Mathematics*, ed by R.B. Braithwaite, (1931) London: Routledge and Keyan Paul, pp. 156-198. Also in *Foundations of Bayesian Decision Theory*, pp. 19-47.

Stohs, M. 1980. "'Uncertainty' in Keynes' General Theory". History of Political Economy 12:372-82.

Stohs, M. 1983. "'Uncertainty' in Keynes' General Theory: a rejoinder". History of Political Economy 15:87-91.

Stove, D. (1967). "Keynes, John Maynard". In the Encyclopedia of Philosophy, ed by Paul Edwards, Vol. 4, 1967, 333-34. London, Macmillan.

Footnotes

[1] Townsend, H. 1988. Letter To Keynes. In Moggridge, ed., 1979, CWJMK, Vol. 29, pp. 289-93.

[2] Keynes, J.M. 1938. Letter to Townsend, ibid, pp. 294-95.

[3] See Gardenfors (1978) for a more advanced treatment that corrects Keynes' analyses and extends it. Note that this section of Keynes' Chapter 14 extends his logic of relevance to incorporate evidence, which does not change the probability value, as an increase in weight of evidence. Thus, if evidence is not irrelevant, it is relevant and w will increase even as p and q do not.

[4] See Keynes (1973), pp. 344-348, especially p. 348, footnote 1 and footnote 2.

[5] Stohs, 1980, p. 378.

[6] By "probable", Keynes means an intermediate degree of probability (see Keynes 1973, p. 127, footnote 1). Uncertainty has nothing to do with the probability relation. "Improbable" means a very low intermediate degree of probability. "Uncertain" means a very low degree of weight; see Keynes: p.

7, 355, 347, 332 ("improbable"); p. 317, 329, 337, 350 ("very improbable"); p. 286 ("vastly improbable"); p. 286 ("not at all improbable"); p. 335 ("no more improbable"); p. 334 ("exceedingly improbable"); p. 201, 202 ("great a priori improbability"). See also pp. 403, 416, 422, 455, 457, 465, and 466.

7   See Keynes (1973), p. 5 ("uncertain"); p. 55, 93 ("uncertainty"); p. 264 ("a finite uncertainty"); p. 294 ("so uncertain"); p. 298 ("an element of uncertainty"); p. 312 (on Hume's use of uncertain); p. 342 ("very uncertain"); and p. 346 ("uncertainty")—used twice; p. 369.

8   Keynes continually emphasized the consistency of his set of definitions throughout the TP. See Keynes (1973), p. 130, especially pp. 37-42, p. 145, p. 157, pp. 171-172 or p. 190, footnote 2 for examples of Keynes' emphasis on correct use of terminology and definition.

9   Keynes, (1973), p. 342.

10   Keynes, (1973), pp. 345-346.

11   See Chapter 3 of the TP, pp. 35-43 for a similar schemization of the probability relation alone.

12   See TP, p. 348, ft. 2 for four examples of Keynes' ordinal quantitative analysis.

13   Stohs, 1983, p. 89.

14   Garner, 1983, p. 85.

15   Stohs, 1980, p. 380; also see Garner, 1983, pp. 85-86 and Stohs, 1983, pp. 89-90.

16   Keynes, 1973, p. 132.

17   Keynes, 1973, pp. 176-177.

18   Keynes, 1973, pp. 177-180. Also see, for example, p. 264 or p. 288.

3

Boole, Keynes and Non-Numerical (Not by a single numeral) Probabilities: An Analysis of Keynes' Interval Estimate Technique

Abstract— John Maynard Keynes was the first logician-philosopher—probability theorist to explicitly set up a rigorous method for working with and calculating interval estimates, as opposed to point estimates. Keynes called this technique "approximation". Approximation underlies Keynes' "finite" probability concept which underlies Part III of the TP on Analogy and Induction. Keynes used the term "non-numerical", which means not by a single numeral, to designate his interval estimate approach. It is based on the original work of George Boole. Keynes corrected Boole's mistakes and adapted Boole's approach to approximation. Keynes then advanced this approach in Part III of the TP by showing how numerical probabilities could be interpreted as upper limits (least upper bounds) for non-numerical probabilities.

1. Introduction

The only references that study the connection between Boole, Keynes, and his interval estimation technique are Brady (1983) and Brady (1993). Levi makes some very general references to Keynes (Levi, 1974, 414-415), but never mentions Keynes' original approach to the use of intervals (non-numerical probabilities) and/or indeterminate probabilities.

> "In virtue of the convexity requirements, both the credence function $Cr_{x,t}(h;e)$ and the confirmation function $c_{x,t}(h;e)$ will take sets of values that are subintervals of the unit line—i.e., the interval from 0 to 1. The lower and upper bounds of such intervals have properties which have been investigated by I.J. Good,[6] C.A.B. Smith,[7] and Dempster.[8]

A partial ordering with respect to comparative credence or with respect to comparative confirmation can be defined as follows:

Def. 3: $(h;e)Cr_{x,t}$ less than or equal to $(h';e')$ if and only if, for every Q-function in $B_{x,t}$, $Q(h;e)$ less than or equal to $Q(h_{\_};e_{\_})$.

Def. 4: $(h;e)Cr_{x,t}$ less than or equal to $(h';e')$ if and only if, for every P-function in $C_{x,t}$, $P(h;e)$ less than or equal to $P(h';e')$.

The partial orderings induced by credal states and confirmational commitments conform to the requirements of B.O. Koopman's axioms for comparative probability.[9] Koopman pioneered in efforts to relax the stringent requirements imposed by bayesians on rational credence. Within the framework of his system, he was able not only to specify conditions of rational comparative probability judgment but to identify ways of generating interval-valued credence functions.

According to Koopman's approach, however, any two credal states (confirmational commitments) represented by the same partial ordering of the elements of M are indistinguishable. My proposal allows for important differences. Several distinct convex sets of probability distributions over the elements of M can induce the same partial ordering on the elements of M according to definitions 3 and 4.

Dempster, Good, Kyburg, Smith, and F. Schick, have all proposed modifying bayesian doctrine by allowing credal states and confimational commitments to be

represented by interval-valued probability functions.[10]"
(Levi, 1974, 406-407).

Levi could have improved on an otherwise excellent article with a simple footnote pointing out that before Koopman's partial ordering and interval estimates analysis, there was Keynes' partial ordering and interval estimates. Keynes was the first. He should receive the credit. The rest of the paper is organized in the following way. Section II presents Keynes' theory of approximation, the construction of interval estimates using not only upper and/or lower limits, but least upper bounds (l.u.b.) and greatest lower bounds (g.l.b.). Section III demonstrates that Keynes made a significant improvement over Boole by defining the existence of "finite" probabilities, so called non-numerical probabilities that have numerical probabiltiies as upper bounds. This approach lies at the heart of Part III of the TP's discussion of analogy and induction. Section IV shows the vast amount of error underlying the queer and strange claims of Guido Fioretti (2003, 2001, 1998). Section V deals with Gay Meek's (2003) strange claims. Section VI conclusion.

2. Keynes and Approximation

"4. Many probabilities—in fact all those which are equal to the probability of some other argument which has the same premiss and of which the conclusion is incompatible with that of the original argument—are numerically measurable in the sense that there is *some* other probability with which they are comparable in the manner described above. But they are not numerically measurable in the most usual sense, unless the probability with which they are thus comparable is the relation of certainty.

.
.
.

Unless, therefore, we are dealing with independent arguments, we cannot apply detailed mathematical reasoning even when the individual probabilities are numerically measurable. The greater part of mathematical probability, therefore, is concerned with arguments which are *both* independent *and* numerically measurable." (Keynes, 1921, 159-160).

Thus, Keynes concludes that

"5. It is evident that the cases in which exact numerical measurement is possible are a very limited class, generally dependent on evidence which warrants a judgment of equi-probability by an application of the Principle of Indifference." (Keynes, 1921, p. 160).

.
.
.

However,

"The sphere of inexact numerical comparison is not, however, quite so limited. Many probabilities, which are incapable of numerical measurement, can be placed nevertheless *between* numerical limits. And by taking particular non-numerical probabilities as standards a great number of comparisons or approximate measurements become possible. If we can place a probability in an order of magnitude with some standard probability, we can obtain its approximate measure by comparison.

This method is frequently adopted in common discourse. When we ask how probable something is, we often put our question in the form—Is it more or less probable than so and so ?—where 'so and so' is some comparable and better known probability. We may thus obtain information in cases where it would be impossible to ascribe any *number* to the probability in question." (Keynes, 1921, p. 160).

The theory of approximation is based on Boole's work, some of which was flawed. However, Keynes' technique incorporates corrections made both by Boole and McCall in later journal literature, as well as by Keynes himself.

> "The theorems given below are chiefly suggested by some work of Boole's. His theorems were introduced for a different purpose, and he does not seem to have realised this interesting application of them; but analytically his problem is identical with that of approximation.[2] This method of approximation is also substantially the same analytically as that dealt with by Mr. Yule under the heading of *Consistence*.[3] (Keynes, 1921, p. 161).

The following two problems are representative of Keynes' approximation technique:

Example 1—
    "(51) xy/h always lies between[1] x/h and $x/h+y/h-1$ and between y/h and $x/h+y/h-1$.

For	$xy/h=x/h-x\acute{y}/h$	By (24.2),
	$=x/h-\acute{y}/h \ x/\acute{y}h$	By X.
Now	$x/\acute{y}h$ lies between 0 and 1 by	(2) and (3),

     _ xy/h lies between x/h and $x/h-\acute{y}/h$,
        i.e. between x/h and $x/h+y/h-1$.

As xy/h_0; the above limits may be replaced by x/h and 0, if $x/h+y/h-1<0$.

We thus have limits for xy/h, close enough sometimes to be useful, which are available whether or not x/h and y/h are *independent* arguments. For instance, if y/h is nearly certain, $xy/h=x/h$ nearly, quite independently of whether or not x and y are independent. This is obvious; but it is useful to have a simple and general formula for all such cases." (Keynes, 1921, p. 162).

[1]In this and the following theorems the term 'between' includes the limits.

Example 2—

"7. It is not worth while to work out more of these results here. Some less systematic approximations of the same kind are given in the course of the solutions in Chapter XVII.

In seeking to compare the degree of one probability with that of another we may desire to get rid of one of the terms, on account of its not being comparable with any of our standard probabilities. Thus our object in general is to eliminate a given symbol of quantity from a set of equations or inequations. If, for instance, we are to obtain numerical limits within which our probability must lie, we must eliminate from the result those probabilities which are non-numerical. This is the general problem for solution."

Example 2¹—

"(55) A general method of solving these problems when we can throw our equations into a linear shape so far as all symbols of probability are concerned, is best shown in the following example:—

Suppose we have

$$\text{lamda} + v = a \tag{i.}$$
$$\text{lamda} + \text{rho} = b \tag{ii.}$$
$$\text{lamda} + v + \text{rho} = c \tag{iii.}$$
$$\text{lamda} + \text{mu} + v + \text{rho} = d \tag{iv.}$$
$$\text{lamda} + \text{mu} + \text{sigma} + \text{tau} = e \tag{v.}$$
$$\text{lamda} + \text{mu} + v + \text{rho} + \text{sigma} + \text{tau} + u = 1 \tag{vi.}$$

where lamda, mu, v, rho, sigma, tau, u represents probabilities which are to be eliminated, and limits are to be found for c in terms of the standard probabilities a, b, d, e, and 1.

Lamda, mu, etc., must all lie between 0 and 1. Hence we have:

Upper limits of c:-b+1-e, a+1-d, a+b (whichever is least); Lower limits of c:-a, b (whichever is greatest).

This example, which is only slightly modified from one given by Boole, represents the actual conditions of a well-known problem in probability." (Keynes, 1921, pp. 162-163).

Keynes devotes pages 86-194, eight plus pages of the TP, to this technique in Chapter 17.

3. Finite Probabilities, Approximation, Analogy, and Induction.

Keynes' major result in Part III of the TP is an advance on Boole's problem X. Keynes gave a corrected version of this on pages 192-194 of the TP. On pages 235-236, Keynes goes beyond Boole:

"Let h represent the general a priori data of the investigation; let g represent the generalization . . . ; let x_1 x_2 . . . x_n represent instances of g.

Then $x_1/gh=1$, $x_2/gh=1$ . . . $x_n/gh=1$; given g. The truth of each instance follows. The problem is to determine the probability g/hx_1x_2 . . . x_n, i.e. the probability of the generalization when n instances of it are given." (Keynes, 1921, p. 235).

Keynes' results are:

"$P_n/P_{n-1} = 1/Y_n$ and hence
$P_n = 1/Y_1Y_2$ . . . $Y_n \cdot P_o$, where $P_o = g/h$, . . ." (Keynes, 1921, p. 235).

and

"$_P_n = . . . = P_o/P_o + X_1X_2$ . . . $X_n/\_h(1-P_o)$.

This approaches unity as a limit, if X_1X_2 . . . $X_n/\_h \cdot (1/P_o)$ approaches zero as a limit, when n increases." (Keynes, 1921, p. 236).

Keynes concludes that

"It follows, therefore, that the probability of an induction tends towards certainty as a limit, when the number of instances is increased, provided that $X_r/X_1X_2 \ldots X_r-1\_h<1-e$ (where Keynes used _ instead of _) for all values of r, and $P_0>\_$, where e and _ are finite probabilities, separated, that is to say, from impossibility by a value of some finite amount, however small. These conditions appear simple, but the meaning of a 'finite probability' requires a word of explanation.[1]

[1]The proof of these conditions, which is obvious, is as follows:

$$X_1X_2 \ldots X_n/\_h=X_n/X_1X_2 \ldots X_{n-1}\_h . X_1X_2 \ldots X_{n-1}/\_h<(1-)^n,$$

where e is finite and $P_0>\_$ where _ is finite. There is always, under these conditions, some finite value of n such that both $(1-e)^n$ and $(1-e)^n/\_$ are less than any given finite quantity, however small." (Keynes, 1921, p. 237).

Keynes then defines "finite probability":

"I argued in Chapter III that not all probabilities have an exact numerical value, and that, in the case of some, one can say no more about their relation to certainty and impossibility than that they fall short of the former and exceed the latter. There is one class of probabilities, however, which I called the numerical class, the ratio of each of whose members to certainty can be expressed by some number less than unity; and we can sometimes compare a non-numerical probability in respect of more and less with one of these numerical probabilities. This enables us to give a definition of 'finite probability' which is capable of application to non-numerical as well as to numerical probabilities. I define a 'finite probability' as one which *exceeds* some numerical probability, the ratio of which to certainty can be expressed by a finite number.[2] The principal method, in which a probability can be proved finite by a process of argument, arises either when its conclusion can be shown to be one of a finite number of alternatives, which are between them exhaustive or, at any rate, have a finite probability, and to which the Principle of Indifference is applicable; or (more usually), when its conclusion is more probable than some hypothesis which satisfies this first condition."

[2]Hence a series of probabilities $P_1 P_2 \ldots P_r$ approaches a limit L, if, given any positive finite number however small, a positive integer n can always be found such that for all values of r greater than n the difference between L and P_r is less than ._, where _ is the measure of certainty." (Keynes, pp. 237-238).

After discussing his conditions of *independent variety* and *finiteness*, Keynes arrives at the following conclusion:

"10. There is a vagueness, it may be noticed, in the number of instances, which would be required on the above assumptions to establish a given numerical degree of probability, which corresponds to the vagueness in the degree of probability which we do actually attach to inductive conclusions. We assume that the necessary number of instances is finite, but we do not know what the number is. We know that the probability of a well-established induction is great, but, when we are asked to name its degree, we cannot. Common sense tells us that some inductive arguments are stronger than others, and that some are very strong. But how much stronger or how strong we cannot express. The probability of an induction is only numerically definite when we are able to make definite assumptions about the number of independent equiprobable influences at work. Otherwise, it is non-numerical, though bearing relations of greater and less to numerical probabilities according to the approximate limits within which our assumption as to the possible number of these causes lies.

11. Up to this point I have supposed, for the sake of
simplicity, that it is necessary to make our assumptions as to
the limitation of independent variety in an absolute form,
to assume, that is to say, the finiteness of the system, to
which the argument is applied, *for certain*. But we need not
in fact go so far as this." (Keynes, 1921, p. 259).

Let us repeat the last part of 10.:

"The probability of an induction is only numerically
definite when we are able to make definite assumptions
about the number of independent equiprobable influences
at work." (Keynes, 1921, p. 259).

Of course, this is exactly a repeat of Keynes' conclusion in
Chapter XV on page 160.

Let us continue.

"Otherwise, it is non-numerical, though bearing
relations of greater and less to numerical probabilities
according to the approximate limits within which our
assumption as to the possible number of these causes lies."
(Keynes, 1921, p. 259).

Of course, "the approximate limits" are derived by means of
Keynes' theory of approximation. Keynes gives the following sources
for approximation in his index. They are

"Boole
•
•
•

and approximation, 161" (Keynes, 1921, p. 459).

and

"Yule (G U Yule-author's note) and approximation,
161." (Keynes, 1921, p. 466).

It is important to note that nowhere in the TP is von Kries ever mentioned in connection with approximation. Further, von Kries' book was only published in 1886. Boole's book was published in 1854. Nowhere in von Kries' book is any systematic interval estimation approach covered.

4. The Strange and Queer Claims of Guido Fioretti.

Fioretti claims that

> "This study suggests that many of Keynes' most noted ideas on uncertainty, such as the existence of non-numerical probabilities . . . date back to Johannes von Kries, 1886." (Fioretti, 1998, p. 150).

This statement is false.
Fioretti claims that

> ". . . the whole of A Treatise on Probability makes it clear that Keynes's 'weights' are not meant as a measure of the sample size. Rather, it is clear that the 'weights' are closely connected to the idea of non-numerical probabilities, which in their turn derive from imperfect analogies." (Fioretti, 2001, p. 258).

This statement is false. If only quantitative information is specified, sample size is a measure of weight. Nor are weights connected to probabilities, numerical or non-numerical. Weight and probability are completely separate concepts analytically.

Fioretti claims that "Although Keynes did recognize his intellectual debt to von Kries, he rejected von Kries' account of non-numerical probabilities." (Fioretti, 2001, p. 260).

Fioretti states, for once correctly, that "even non-numerical probabilities are limited by numerical lower and upper bounds." (Fioretti, 2001, p. 268). Of course, such bounds (intervals) are calculated on the basis of Keynes Theory of approximation, which is based on Boole. Nowhere, in any of Fioretti's articles, is Boole's and/or Keynes' theory of approximation mentioned. Fioretti quotes Keynes' major conclusion (Keynes, 1921, p. 259; 1973, p. 288) in Fioretti, p. 267. However, Fioretti has *no* idea or clue of what Keynes is doing since the concepts of finite probability and approximation are *necessary* prerequisites.

Fioretti makes other errors. For instance,

> "The 'weights of arguments' must entail both issues. According to Runde (1990), it is even possible to identify two sorts of weights in Keynes' writings." (Fioretti, p. 268).

Fioretti simply accepts the error-filled work of Runde (1990). Fioretti also accepts the error-filled paper of Allin Cottrell, 1993 as a basis for his paper. (Fioretti, p. 269).

Fioretti claims

> "An important aspect of the story of the development of Keynes's ideas was his discovery of Johannes von Kries, a German logician and neuro-physiologist who came to the idea that probabilities are in general non-comparable and non-numerical. Keynes was quite open about this source of inspiration but, at the time he was writing *A Treatise on Probability*, attempted to accomodate von Kries's non-numerical probabilities into an unsuitable philosophical framework, one which he later rejected.
>
> Going back to von Kries is extremely useful when attempting to clarify the concept of non-numerical probability in *A Treatise on Probability* (CWVIII), as well as the continuities and discontinuities between the *Treatise* and *The General Theory of Employment, Interest, and Money* (CWVII)." (Fioretti, 2003, p. 130).

Nowhere in the *TP* can anything like Fioretti's claims be found. Fioretti claims that

> ". . . probabilities are not numerical. However, according to Keynes, finiteness of possible qualities permits constraining

non-numerical probabilities within numerical lower and
upper bounds (ibid.: 288)." (Fioretti, p. 134).

This conclusion follows only if Fioretti is aware, which he is
not, of Keynes' theory of approximation and definition of "finite"
probability, both of which, directly or indirectly, come from George
Boole in 1854 and not von Kries in 1886. The idea that Keynes
would accept a mediocre thinker like von Kries over George Boole
is ludicrous.

Fioretti finishes by proclaiming utter nonsense:

> "Studying von Kries undoubtedly helps us to
> understand Keynes's seemingly awkward statements
> concerning non-numerical probabilities. Furthermore, it
> throws light on current models of 'fundamental' uncertainty
> (Fioretti 1998). However, von Kries is also a good starting
> point for improving on Keynes's thought, both with respect
> to individual as well a sto collective behaviour." (Fioretti,
> 2003, p. 139).

There is nothing written by J. Von Kries that would help "us
to understand Keynes's seemingly awkward statements concerning
non-numerical probabilities." (Fioretti, 2003, p. 139).

I conclude that Guido Fioretti is simply a mathematical, statistical,
and probabilistic innumerant. All his articles are simply nonsense in
general. Those parts which are correct are small in comparison.

5. The Strange and Queer Claims of Gay Meek.

She states the following:

> "1. The original version of this chapter was completed
> in 1976, widely circulated in Cambridge and beyond, and
> used in seminars and a graduate lecture series. (Anna Carabelli
> was already working on an allied topic; similar lines of
> thinking on rational behaviour subsequently appeared in
> O'Donnell (thesis and 1989) and in Lawson (1985); and

Coddington (1982) took a hostile but lively line (without direct reference to my work) on the points I made about scepticism and uncertainty.) The essay, slightly revised, was then published by Cambridge University Press in Thoughtful Economic Man (Meeks 1991): further backing for and discussion of the analysis presented here can be found in that considerably longer piece." (Meeks, 2003, p. 34).

This footnote reveals Meeks to be another major error generator, much like Runde. A. Carabelli's (1988) and R. O'Donnell's (1989) severe misrepresentation of non-numerical probabilities, based on a complete misunderstanding of Keynes' diagram on page 39 (Keynes, 1921, p. 39; 1973, p. 42) of the TP can now be traced back to Meeks:

"On this anaylsis, although 'some inductive arguments are stronger than others and . . . some are very strong', still 'how much stronger or how strong we cannot express' (ibid.: 288, see also 30-1). Ordinal ranking of probabilities will sometimes be elusive too (as in comparing propositions each based on a different type of evidence; ibid.: 31-2).[14] Nor is it always possible even to make comparisons with a 50:50 benchmark:

Is our expectation of rain, when we start out for a walk, always *more* likely . . . or *less* likely . . . or *as* likely as not? I am prepared to argue that on some occasions *none* of these alternatives hold . . . If the barometer is high, but the clouds are black, it is not always rational that one should prevail over the other in our minds, or even that we should balance them . . . (ibid.: 32).

There is much more to Keynes's analysis of probability (for the full story, see CWVIII, especially Part I, Chapter 3).[15] (Meeks, 2003, p. 30).

Meeks starts out referring to Section 10 of Chapter XXII of the TP on page 259 (Keynes, 1921, p. 259; 1973, p. 288). However, she leaves out, in fact, deliberately ignores, the fact that upper-lower bounds (intervals) can be constructed based on Keynes' Boolean approach to approximation. Of course, it is not possible to compare or rank intervals *if they overlap*, which is Keynes' point in the cloud-barometer example quoted by Meeks.

Finally, while "there is much more to Keynes' analysis of probability" (Meeks, 2003, p. 30) in Chapters 15, 16, and 17 of the TP and much more to Keynes' analysis of induction and analogy in Chapters 20-22 of the TP, the full story will definitely *not be found* "especially (in) Part I, Chapter 3" of CWJMK, Volume VII. (Meeks, 2003, p. 30).

Meeks' fundamental error is to claim that a study of Keynes'diagram (1973, p. 42) allows one to understand Keynes' concept and application of non-numerical probability. Chapter III of Part I of the TP is an *introductory* chapter. Just as Paul Davidson and the rest of the post Keynesian, Institutionalist and Cambridge Keynesians concentrate on Chapter 3, Book I, of the GT, an introductory chapter, so Gay Meeks bases her entire framework on an introduction, which has no theory of approximation or finite probabilities.

6. The Ignorance of I. Levi, H.E. Kyburg, Jr., and H.E. Smokler.

A reader of R. Samuelson's *Newsweek* column would no doubt argue that shoddy, shabby, and holely analysis should be expected from economists, who are, after all, not scientists. Such work would no doubt be discounted in the writings of scientists, logicians, and philosophers of science specializing in the fields of probability, statistics, and logic. Unfortunately, this is not the case. The same very poor scholarship and errors appear in, for example, the work of I. Levy, H.E. Kyburg, and H.E. Smokler.

Consider the following false claim made by Kyburg and Smokler:

> "The idea of upper and lower probabilities, first developed for a logical interpretation of probability by Kyburg, has been independently developed in one form or

another by various writers on subjective probability in addition to Smith: Good,[55] Shafer,[56] Dempster,[57] and others. (Kyburg and Smokler, 1980, p. 18.)

Obviously, neither Kyburg or Smokler ever read Chapters 6-21 of Boole's 1854 classic, *The Laws of Thought* or got past Chapter 6 of J.M. Keynes' *TP*. It is J.M. Keynes, basing his approach on Boole, who developed the idea of upper and lower probabilities, period! Now, jump ahead 21 years to I. Levi. He claims that

"Prior to the early 1970's, Ellsberg's discussion of decision-making when probabilities go indeterminate or "ambiguous" is the most comprehensive discussion of which I am aware.[2]

[2]There had been important discussions of indeterminate probability without special reference to decision-making in Koopman (1940), Kyburg (1961), and Good (1962). Discussions of indeterminate probability that do consider its impact on decision-making include, in particular, Good (1952), Hurwicz (1951), Hodges and Lehmann (1952), Smith (1961) and Wald (1942, 1947, and 1950).

(Levi, 2001, p. 10.)

and

"The first prong points to work by authors such as Koopman (1940) and Good (1952, 1962) who proposed formal theories of probability that allow for interval—valued probability judgment based on the testimony of deliberating agents concerning their comparative judgments of probability in addition to their testimony concerning their choice behavior in actual and hypothetical contexts of choice.

. . . The second prong of Ellsberg's argument appeals to Smith's account of upper and lower probabilities (Smith

> 1961), which purports to invoke only data of the
> "behavioralist" variety to elicit such probabilities. We are
> entitled to entertain the suggestion that the interval-valued
> probabilities of Koopman and Good coincide with the
> interval values determined by Smith's upper and lower
> "pignic" probabilities." (Levi, 2001, p. 17.)

Obviously, Levi is unaware that the most comprehensive discussion of interval estimates, upper-lower probabilities and "ambiguity" appears in J.M. Keynes' *TP*. Further, it is in the work of Hailperin that the Keynes-Boole approach was simplified into a much easier linear programming approach.

Ellsberg himself (Ellsberg, 2001) simply fills in the above pattern. Throughout his book, the idea of interval estimates and/ or upper-lower probabilities is credited to Good and Koopman, not Keynes and Boole.

A crucial failing of Ellsberg, Kyburg, Levi, Ramsey, etc., is their failure to read beyond Chapters 4-6 of the *TP*. This approach mimics the approach of how economists, such as Joan Robinson, Richard Kahn, Sydney Weintraub, Paul Davidson, and Dennis Robertson, read the GT. Chapters 1-3 supposedly supply the ecomonist with the core of Keynes' Theory of Effective Demand. Of course, Keynes' Theory of Effective Demand is contained, fully modeled and explained, in Chapters 20 and 21 of the GT. Similarly, Chapters 5, 10, 15, 17, 26, 29, and 30 of the *TP* contain Keynes' work on the topics discussed in this section concerning the *TP*.

7. Conclusion

The conclusion reached is that not only Meeks, but the vast majority of economists doing work in the fields of economic thought, history of economic thought, economic history, methodology of economics, philosophy of economics, post Keynesian economics, Institutionalist and English neo-Keynesian economics are logically, mathematically, statistically, and probabilistically inept and innumerant. Economists like Meeks,

O'donnell, Carabelli, Fitzgibbons, Runde, Fioretti, etc., could not possibly understand Keynes' concept of approximation or finite probability because they can't follow the logical mathematical exposition. Ignorance is bliss. How much easier it is to proclaim an introductory chapter with a simple diagram as the alpha and omega of Keynes' logical theory of probability than to take a course in advanced calculus and/or Boolean logic and algebra in order to prepare oneself for the difficult journey of mastering the work of a genius. This, of course, would take too much time and effort. It is much easier to assert without evidence that Keynes was "anti-mathematical" and against "formalism".

References

Baioletti, M., Capotorti A., Tulipani, S. And B. Vantaggi (2000). "Elimination of Boolean Variables for Probabilistic Coherence", Soft Computing, 4, 81-88.

Boole, George (1854). The Laws of Thought. New York: Dover.

Brady, Michael E. (1983). The Logical Foundations of Keynes' Macroeconomics: His Logical Theory of Probability and its Application in the General Theory. (Unpublished doctoral dissertation, U.C. Riverside) University of Michigan: Microfilms International.

Brady, Michael E. (1993). "J.M. Keynes' Theoretical Approach to Decision-Making Under Conditions of Risk and Uncertainty", Brit. J. For the Phil. Of Sci, 44, 357-376.

Ellsberg, D. (2001). Risk, Ambiguity and Decision. New York, Garland Publishing, Inc.

Fioretti, G. (2003). "No Faith, No Conversion . . .". In Runde and Mizuhara, 2003, 130-139.

Fioretti, G. (2001). "Von Kries and the Other German Logicians' -Non-Numerical Probabilities Before Keynes", Economics and Philosophy, 17, 245,273.

Fioretti, G. (1998). "John Maynard Keynes and Johannes von Kries", History of Economic Ideas, 6, 51-80.

Hansen, P., Jaumard, B., and M.P. de Aragao (1995). "Boole's Conditions of Possible Experience and Reasoning Under Uncertainty", Discrete Applied Mathematics, 60, 181-193.

Keynes, J.M. (1921). A Treatise on Probability. London: Macmillan (AMS Reprint ed., 1979).

Keynes, J.M. (1973). A Treatise on Probability. Volume VIII of the CW@JMK London: Macmillan.

Kyburg, H.E. and Smokler, H.E. (1980). Studies in Subjective Probability. Krieger Publishing Co., Inc. 2nd Edition.

Kyburg, H.E. and Smokler, H.E. (1980). "Introduction". In Studies in Subjective Probability. Krieger Publishing Co., Inc. 2nd Edition.

Levi, I. (2001). "Introduction". In D. Ellsberg, Risk, Ambiguity and Decision. 2001. New York, Garland Publishing, Inc.

Levi, Issac. (1974). "Indeterminate Probabilities", The Journal of Philosophy, 71, 391-418.

Meeks, G.T. (2003). "Keynes on the Rationality of Decision Procedures Under Uncertainty: The Investment Decision". In Runde and Mizuhara, 2003, 196-204.

Runde, J. And Mizuhara, S., ed. (2003). The Philosophy of Keynes's Economics: Probability, Uncertainty, and Convention. New York: Routledge.

Samuelson, R.J. (2001). "The Illusion of Knowledge. If you're inclined to think that most economists are clueless-well, you might actually be right", Newsweek, May 21 p. 49.

Samuelson, R.J. (2002). "Optimists—or Just Dreamers". Economic forecasters maybe deluding themselves if they are counting on a quick, strong recovery." Newsweek, January 14, p. 39.

Footnote

[1]   There is a minor problem of exposition with the diagram on page 39 of the TP (p. 42 of 1973 CWJMK editing, Volume 8). Two diagrams, not one, were needed. Keynes' diagram shows *non-linear* functions. The dash masks and/or intersection points of intersecting curves delineate where intervals

can serve as bounds. Given Keynes' concern with non-linear probability preferences, as exhibited by a two or three dimensional analysis of his conventional coefficient of risk and weight, c, the diagram is ok. It could also hueristically represent the type of problem worked out by Keynes on pages 186-194, where the probabilities are roots of nth order equations. However, both of the example problems are *linear* in the probabilities. Thus, a second diagram, composed of *linear* line segments, would have, from hindsight of 60 years, been a helpful pedogogical device. It would also have helped to see a footnote on page 39 stating "see Chapters XV, XVI, and XVII".

4

An Analysis of the Failure of SIPTA, the Economics Profession, and the Philosophy Profession to Deal with the Upper-Lower Probability Interval Estimate Approaches of Boole, Keynes, and Hailperin

Abstract— A representative sample of SIPTA (Society for Imprecise Probability Theory and Application) Literature is examined. Boole and T. Hailperin are never mentioned. J.M. Keynes is mentioned in throw-away one liners or specifically cited only in relation to the first four Chapters of the *TP*. This is precisely identical to the F.P. Ramsey approach to reading the *TP*, which was to read only Chapters 1-4 of the TP plus a scattering of 10-15 pages taken from the remaining 29 Chapters of the *TP*. Such an approach is doomed to failure. Modern day examples of this approach are in Runde, Fioretti, and Weatherson.

1. Boole and Keynes

B oole's upper-lower probability approach starts at the beginning of Chapter 16 of his *The Laws of Thought* (1854) and ends in Chapter 21. Keynes builds on Boole in his *A Treatise on Probability* (*TP*). In a footnote at the start of Chapter 5 of the

TP, appropriately titled "Other Methods of Determining Probabilities", Keynes states:

> "Parts of Chapter 15 are closely connected with the topics of the following paragraphs, and the discussion which is commenced here is concluded there." (Keynes, 1921, p. 65.)

In the last section of Chapter 10, Section 7, Keynes states:

> "In Chapter 15 I bring the non-numerical theory of probability developed in the preceding chapters into connection with the usual numerical conception of it, and demonstrate how and in what class of cases a meaning can be given to a numerical measure . . . . This leads on to what may be termed numerical approximation . . . the relating of probabilities, which are not themselves numerical, to probabilities, which are numerical, by means of *greater* or *less*, by which in some cases numerical limits may be ascribed to probabilities which are not capable of numerical measures." (Keynes, 1921, p 122.)

Of course, on page 161 of Chapter 15, Keynes makes it crystal clear that his method of approximation is based primarily on Boole's work. Keynes also gives Yule a reference.

Keynes then applies this approach on pages 162-163 and on pages 186-194 of the *TP*. The reader should note that Keynes uses a revised version of Boole's problem X (Laws of Thought, p. 358) on which to construct his analysis of induction and analogy in Part III of the *TP* (see pages 235-238 and pages 254-255). Keynes' approach is thus an improved and upgraded version of Boole.

Unfortunately, with the exceptions of Russell, Carnap, Brady (1993, 1994, 2002), and Brady and Nauman (2003), this entire discussion has been ignored. For instance, Runde and Mizuhara (2003) support Fioretti's hilarious claim that Keynes' analysis is based on Von Kries!! Of course, there is not a shred of evidence to support his delusion. Weatherson relies on SIPTA articles and suggests that Keynes' "strange, mysterious" non-numerical probabilities can be interpreted as if they were interval estimates. Since they *are* interval estimates, Weatherson's argument illustrates his failure to read Chapters 5, 10, 15, and 17 of the *TP*, among others.

2. T. Hailperin

Hailperin made a series of break throughs. He showed (see references) how the Boole-Keynes type problem could be reformulated as a linear programming problem and solved using the simplex method and/or other more-advanced algorithms. Specifically, integer and mixed integer programming techniques allow for a much easier way of formulating and solving interval estimate probability problems. The linear programming approach was later also used by researchers in the fields of fuzzy logic and possibility theory.

3. Kyburg, SIPTA, and J.M. Keynes

The first thing to note is that references to Boole and T. Hailperin are non-existent in Kyburg (1998-2000, 2003), Regoli (1998-2000), Smithson (1997-2000), and Walley (1997-98, 1997-2000).

Keynes gets a few one line references that do not alert the reader to the historical fact that Keynes had an EXPLICIT approach, called approximation, for the construction of upper-lower probabilities, limits, bounds, or intervals.

Kyburg gives Keynes credit for recognizing the existence of partial orders only. However, all other evalutions of Keynes' work is screwed up by Kyburg. Supposedly,

> "He did not provide a mathematical structure for his probability values [but] he did give us some hints." [Kyburg, 1998-2000, p. 1].

and

> "Keynes' ideas were taken up by B.O. Koopman . . ." (Kyburg, 1998-2000, p.2.)

and

> ". . . interval valued probabilities . . . seem to conform
> to Keynes' intuitions." (Kyburg, 1998-2000, p. 2.)

In the first issue of the SIPTA Newsletter, Kyburg again gives Keynes credit for the partially ordered concept (Kyburg 2003, p. 3), citing (Keynes, 1921, p. 28, 30, 34) but it was

> "Bernard Koopman, who provides an elegant
> axiomatization of Keynes' ideas . . . and introduces upper
> and lower probabilities explicitly . . ." (Kyburg, ibid., p. 3.)

Kyburg has it all wrong. Keynes' mathematical structure is an improved version of Boole's mathematical structure. Contrary to Kyburg, Keynes didn't just have "ideas" and "intuitions" that lacked "explicit" mathematical-modeling. Long before Kyburg was born, Keynes had presented an advanced mathematical technique for the calculation (approximation) of upper and lower probabilities.

> P. Achinstein's assessment of Keynes is even worse. In
> his latest book, he states the following: "I end this section
> with a quote from John Maynard Keynes, whose book on
> probability contains lots of insights" (2001, p. 226). Of
> course, this is the same type of shoddy assessment contained
> in Levi and Kyburg.

4. Frank Ramsey, the economists, and John Maynard Keynes

The economics literature is essentially based on the extremely flimsy and shoddy "analysis" of Keynes' approach to measurement contained on pages 26-32 of Ramsey (1980), primarily in a section titled "Mr. Keynes' Theory". Ramsey commits many errors in these pages, such as,

> "But if, as Mr. Keynes holds, these things are not always
> expressible by numbers . . ." (Ramsey, p. 27)

"Indeed some of his arguments against their numerical
measurement . . ." (Ramsey, p. 27).

". . . that, as Mr. Keynes thinks, to the non-numerical
probability relation corresponds a non-numerical degree of
rational belief . . ." (Ramsey, p. 27).

Sadly, Ramsey presents a caricature of "Mr. Keynes' Theory".
It is clear that Ramsey bases his *whole* assessment of Keynes' views
on measurement on his queer reading of Chapter 3 of the *TP* alone.
Ramsey completely ignores Keynes' analysis in Chapters 5, 10,
15, 17, and Parts 3, 4, and 5 of the *TP*, where Keynes develops his
interval approach based on a modification of Boole's work. Keynes
calls his interval approach "approximation" (Keynes, 1921, pages
159-161). This immediately calls into question the false claim of
Kyburg and Smokler that Kyburg was the first to develop the idea
of upper and lower probabilities for a logical interpretation of
probability (see Kyburg, Jr., and Smokler, 1980, p. 18).

Given Keynes' clear-cut analysis in Chapter 5, Chapter 10,
section 7, and Chapters 15 and 17 of the *TP*, the Keynesian Theory
of measuring probabilities is the following:

(a) If symmetrical evidence exists, probabilities can be
measured by a single numeral (number). They are numerical
probabilities based on the principle of indifference and/or
a uniform/rectangular probability distribtuion.

(b) If non symmetrical evidence exists, probabilities can be
measured by using *two* numerals. They are "non-numerical"
because *two*, not *one*, numerals are required. These are
intervals.

(c) However, a problem exists concerning the comparison of
intervals. If there is *any* overlap between two intervals, it is
not possible to say that one of the two is greater than, less
than, or equal to the other. Thus, the problem is one of
comparison, not one of *measurability*.

This error[1] of Ramsey's, his talking about Keynes' concept of
intervals (approximation) as if they were some mysterious "non-
numerical" platonic entities was also committed 50 years later by

Stohs (1980, 1983) and Garner (1983). It was then incorporated into a vast and growing economics literature on Keynes' *TP* from 1983-2003. The reader should take a look at any of the following articles or books—Baddeley (1999), Bateman (1987, 1988, 1991, 1995), Carabelli (1988, 1995, 1998, 2002), Coates (1996), Cottrell (1993), Davis (1994), Dow and Dow (1985), Dow (1993), Dow and Hilliard (1995), Fioretti (1998, 2001), Fitzgibbons (1988), Gerrard (1994), Gillies, D. And I. Gillies (1991), Lawson (1985, 1987), McCann (1994), Marchionatti (1999), Meeks (1991), O'Donnell (1989, 1991), Runde (1990, 1991, 1994a, 1994b, 1994c, 1995), Weatherson (2002), and Winslow (1986, 1989, 1995).

This, of course, leads us to Runde and Mizuhara's (2003) collection of 19 articles by many of the same so-called "experts" that I have listed above.

For example, McCann (see McCann, pages 43-44, Runde and Mizuhara, 2003) badly misquotes section 7 of Keynes' Chapter 10 of the *TP*, deliberately leaving out Keynes' references to Chapter 15 and his theory of approximation. Fioretti makes totally unsupportable claims such as his claim that J. Von Kries is the source of Keynes' "non-numerical" probability approach and that it "is extremely useful when attempting to clarify the concept of non-numerical probability in A Treatise on Probability" to go back "to Von Kries" (see Fioretti, p. 130, Runde and Mizuhara, 2003). The only reference to Von Kries in Chapters 5, 10, 15, and 17 of the *TP* is on page 67 (1921). It has nothing to do with Keynes' Theory of Approximation based on the work of the English genius George Boole.

5. The Blunders of Bradley Bateman— An Example of Innumeracy

Instead of Bateman, I could of used Carabelli, O'Donnell, Davis, Runde, Fioretti, Winslow, etc., as my example. What is common for this entire group of economists is that they are well-meaning, but ill-trained amateurs. They do not have the tools to comprehend or understand Keynes' technical analysis. They are mathematically, statistically, and logically illiterate. The reader should note that Levi, Kyburg, Jr., and Achinstein do not have this excuse. Let us first outline the technical steps used by Keynes to arrive at his conclusions concerning analogy and induction in Chapter 20 of the *TP*.

First, in a footnote at the beginning of Chapter 5 of the *TP*, titled "Other Methods of Determining Probabilities", Keynes informs the reader that "parts of Chapter 15 are closely connected" to the discussion in Chapter 5 and "the discussion which is commenced here is concluded there". No economist, Bateman included, has read Chapter 5 of the *TP* (or Chapters 10, 15, 17, 29-32).

Second, in section 7 of Chapter 10, Keynes states that "In Chapter 15, I bring the non-numerical theory of probability . . . into connection with the usual numerical conception of it . . . . This leads on to what may be termed numerical approximation . . . by which in some cases numerical limits may be ascribed to probabilities which are not capable of numerical measure" (Keynes 1921, p. 122).

Third, in Chapter 15 Keynes states "many probabilities which are incapable of numerical measurement, can be placed nevertheless *between* numerical limits. And by taking particular non-numerical probabilities as standards a great number of comparisons or approximate measurements become possible" (Keynes, 1921, p. 160).

Fourth, "most of such comparisons must be based on . . . Chapter 5. But it is possible . . . to develop a systematic method of approximation which may be occasionally useful. The same assessment is made with respect to the use of Tchebycheff's Inequality—"Tchebycheff's more cautious limits may sometimes prove useful" (Keynes, 1921, p. 356)-author's note]. The theorems given below are chiefly suggested by some work of Boole's".

Fifth, Keynes proceeds to demonstrate his method of approximation on pages 162-163, 186-194 of the *TP*. Of great importance is "Boole's problem 10" (Keynes, 1921, p. 192) because "the same problem . . . will be discussed in dealing with pure induction" (Keynes, 1921, p. 192, ft.1).

Sixth, this modified problem appears as the *central proof* in Chapter 20 of the *TP* on pages 235-236 of Keynes approach to analog.

Seventh, this result requires the existence of finite probabilities (Keynes, 1921, p. 237).

> "Those conditions appear simple, but the meaning of a
> 'finite probability' requires a word of explanation".

Thus, ". . . we can sometimes compare a non-numerical probability (i.e., an interval; author's note) in respect to more or less with one of these numerical probabilities. This enables us to give a definition of 'finite probability' which is capable of application to non-numerical as well as to numerical probabilities. I define a 'finite probability' as one which *exceeds* some numerical probability . . ." (Keynes, 1921, p. 237).

Eighth, Keynes expands the Chapter 20 discussion into Chapter 22 on pages 254-259. In section 10 of Chapter 22, Keynes states:

> "The probability of an induction is only numerically
> definite when we are able to make definite assumptions
> about the number of equiprobable influences at work.
> Otherwise, it is non-numerical (i.e., an interval; author's
> note), though hearing relations of greater and less to
> numerical probabilities according to the approximate limits
> within which our assumption as to the possible number of
> these causes lies" (Keynes, 1921, p. 259).

We can now conclude that without an understanding of "approximation" and "finite probabilities", Part 3 of the *TP* can't be understood. Of course, underlying these concepts is Boole's original upper-lower limits approach. However, none of the economists (or philosophers) cited in the references ever cites or even mentions Boole, approximation, finite probabilities, Chapter 5, Chapter 10, Chapter 15, Chapter 17, Chebyshev's Inequality, etc., a single time.

Bradley Bateman (BB) covers Keynes' modification of Boole's problem 10 in (Bateman 1987, pages 101-103) and (Bateman, 1990, pages 363-366). However, he completely overlooks the interval estimate nature of Keynes' probability theory. No operational significance is shown to follow from Keynes' discussion. He attempts to link Part 3 to Part 5 of the *TP*. On page 368, his claim, with respect to Tchebycheff, that Keynes criticised him for making unwarranted assumptions, is simply false. Keynes praised Tchebycheff for providing *a general* theorem from which the results of Bernoulli (binomial), Laplace, Poisson, and Czuber are special cases. Again, BB is unable to show how Keynes operationalized the application side of his logical theory of probability.

BB is at his worst, however, in his frequent claims that Keynes "capitulated" to the criticisms made by Ramsey in 1922 and 1926 and adopted a subjective *theory* of probability because such a theory was operational, in a 1931 eulogy to Ramsey (Bateman, 1991, pages 102, 105, 106, 107, 109; 1994, 101, 102, 103, 104). Keynes theory of logical probability is objective at the theoretical level, since it adds the additional constraint that beliefs are *rational*, as opposed to subjective probability where beliefs are weak or strong. At the applied level, however, probability is subjective given all the information, time, and skill constraints. Only the logical relation of partial entailment is objective. The operation of estimating a probability is relative to incomplete data, information or knowledge. Only in the extreme case where Keynes' index for the weight of evidence, w, equals 1 and the decision maker understands the correct model of the decision context would Ramsey's point be sound. More importantly, Keynes rejected Ramsey's approach as a foundation for induction and analogy at the end of his eulogy. Note that Ramsey himself had great difficulty in understanding the difference between *theory* and application. Ramsey never got beyond Chapter 3 of the TP. All of a sudden, Ramsey is confronted, on page 32 of the *TP* (1921), by Keynes' statements that "probability is . . . relative . . . to the principles of *human* reason . . .

is relative in part to the secondary propositions . . . relative to human powers" (Keynes, 1921, p. 32).

Ramsey claims,

> "This passage seems to me quite unreconcilable with the view which Mr. Keynes adopts everywhere except in this . . . passage" (Ramsey, 1980, p. 29).

Unfortunately, the "everywhere" for Ramsey is Chapter 3 of the *TP*, read in isolation from the rest of the book. Ramsey needed to read Parts 2, 3, 4, and 5 of the *TP* to give a serious review.

Finally, BB commits the error of confusing the question of measurability with the question of comparability. All probabilities are measurable by either one numeral or two for Keynes. However, many probabilities are not comparable due to overlap in the intervals (Bateman, 1991, p. 106).

6. Correcting the Errors of E. Roy Weintraub, Mark Stohs, and C. Alan Garner.

> "In Chapter 8 of *A Treatise on Probability*, Keynes rejected the relative frequency theory, since "if we allow it to hold the field. We must admit that probability is *not* the guide to life, and in following it we are not acting according to reason" (Weintraub, 1975, p. 531).

Of course, J.M. Keynes *DID NOT* reject the relative frequency theory. He rejected *Venn's* relative frequency theory—

> "Venn's theory by itself has few practical applications, and if we allow it to hold the field, we must admit that probability is *not* the guide to life, and that in following it we are not acting according to reason" (Keynes, 1921, p. 96; incorrectly cited by Weintraub using the 1973 CWJMK edition of the *TP*, page 102).

Keynes' argument is that all relative frequency theories, even the vastly improved relative frequency/logical hybrid he proposed in Chapter 8 of the *TP*, are special theories while his logical theory is the general theory (Keynes, 1921, pages 98, 104).

Further,

> "We should not overlook the element of truth which the frequency theory embodies and which provides its plausibility. In the first place, it gives a true account, so long as it does not argue that probability and frequency are *identical*, of a large number of the most *precise* arguments in probabiliy . . ."

> "In the second place, the statement that the probability of an event is measured by its actual frequency of occurrence 'in the long run' has a very close connection with a valid conclusion which can be derived *in certain cases*, from Bernoulli's Theorem" (Keynes, 1921, p. 109).

Keynes then directs the reader to Part 5, Chapter 29, of the *TP*. In Chapter 29, the reader will find that Keynes favors Chebyshev's Inequality as the general case for application with the normal and binomial (Bernoulli) distributions considered special cases whose applicability must be examined in a case by case basis.

I have spent some time on Weintraub's very poor scholarship because it is a good representative sample of the very poor scholarship done by economists who attempt to read the *TP* in a piece meal fashion a-la Frank Ramsey. Stohs and Garner, however, are even worse.

Stohs section 4 on "probability calculations" is an awful mess. First, Stohs claims,

> "It can be argued than, that Keynes consistently argues against the attempt to use a Benthamite type of probability calculus in determining prospective yields. He does not deny that some sort of calculation can be made. We might wonder, though, whether this distinction has any further basis in

Keynes' works. The majority of Chapter 3 of his *Treatise on Probability* is devoted to denying the two assumptions made by a Benthamite type of probability calculus. Further, the distinction between those probabilities that are numerically expressible and comparable and those which are not is emphasized in the summary of the first part of the *Treatise*.

We wish, that is to say, to have a numerical measure of degrees of probability.

This is only occasionally possible. A rule can be given for numerical measurement when the conclusion is one of a number of equiprobable, exclusive, and exhaustive alternatives, but not otherwise.[26]

Given such evidence, we are justified in holding to the suggested interpretation of these issues. One problem is that Keynes does not specify in the *General Theory* how we are to carry out the probability calculations of prospective yields. We can assume, at least, that these would be non-numerical calculations." (Stohs, 1980, pages 379-380).

Stohs, like Ramsey, concentrates on Chapter 3 of the *TP* alone. Stohs has no idea of what an interval estimate is. His talk about non-numerical calculations is absurd.

Garner then gets into the act in a 1983 comment:

"A second comment relates to the quotation in Stohs' article at the bottom of page 378. Stohs has quoted correctly a reprint in Harris of Keynes' 1937 article, but, unfortunately, the reprint is wrong.[4] The version in Harris reads, "About these matters there is no scientific basis on which to form any capable probability whatever", and Stohs emphasized the word 'capable' when arguing that Keynes believed that some type of probability calculation is possible. In the original article, Keynes wrote ". . . any calculable probability whatever". This difference undercuts Stohs' conclusion that "the passage does not state that no probability calculation whatsoever can be made".[5] However, what did Keynes mean by the word 'calculable'? It seems clear that he ruled out numerical probability calculations, but what about Stohs' 'non-numerical calculations'? Indeed, what is a non-numerical probability calculation?" (Garner, 1983, p. 84).

Garner is simply ignorant about the concept of interval estimate. Stohs' reply shows that his reading of the *TP* is, like Ramsey's limited to Chapter 3 primarily plus some piecemeal fishing expeditions:

> "That the investor *has* low confidence about prospective yield calculations suggested that these calculations are actually carried out. Garner's second comment is that Keynes claims that there is no basis for forming "any *calculable* probability whatever" (my emphasis).[14] How then can such calculations be carried out?
>
> In *UKGT* it was suggested that these calculations are carried out on a non-numerical (i.e., psychological or intuitive) basis. Garner apparently believes that this suggestion is mine, for he says that it "seems clear that [Keynes] rules out numerical probability calculations, but what about Stohs' "non-numerical calculations"?[15] But this suggestion originates with Keynes' work, as is clear from his *Treatise on Probability*:
>
> The recognition of the fact, that not all probabilities are numerical, limits the scope of the Principle of Indifference. It has always been agreed that a numerical measure can actually be obtained in those cases only in which a reduction to a set of exclusive and exhaustive *equiprobable* alternatives is practicable.[16]
>
> It should be quite clear that prospective yield calculations would be non-numerical in nature. If one reads Keynes' claim that there is no basis for forming "any *calculable* probability whatever" as the claim that there is no basis for a *numerical* probability, then it is clear that Keynes would allow that non-numerical calculations about prospective yield probabilities can be carried out.

[15] Ibid. Garner also asks for an explanation of this non-numerical notion of probability. Keynes never fully explained this notion, and an attempt on my part would require a separate article. But see the *General theory*, pp. 162-63, and *A Treatise on probability* (London, 1921), ch. 3. It is possible that Keynes would have welcomed Shackle's analysis in terms of potential surprise and ascendancy; see Garner 1983, n. 8." (Garner, 1983, pages 89-90).

Stohs ends his article in an intellectual quagmire, arguing for the development of "Keynes' notion of a non-numerical probability", (Stohs, 1983, p. 91).

Contrary to Garner and Stohs, Keynes fully explained his "notion" of a "non-numerical probability" (an interval estimate) in Chapters 5, 10, 15, and 17 of the *TP*. He showed how such an approach could serve as a foundation for induction and analogy in Chapters 20 and 22 of the *TP*. He showed how one could use his decision rule (conventional coefficient of weight and risk) in Chapter 26, as well as advocating the use of Chebyshev's Inequality in Chapter 29. Finally, Keynes argued that one could use a relative frequency-normal distribution approach *if* the data passed the Lexis Q Test in Chapter 32 of the *TP*. However, the answer *will not* be found on pages 162-163 of the GT or in Chapter 3 of the *TP*, as claimed by Stohs. Nor does non-numerical translate as on a "(i.e., psychological or intuitive) basis" (Stohs, 1983, p. 89) or "rules of thumb" or "heuristics" (Garner, 1983, 85)[1]. For Keynes, non-numerical mean "not by one number", but two.

6. Conclusions

Kyburg's view that Keynes' intuitions and ideas in the *TP* served as an inspiration for other researchers to later develop the explicit mathematical, logical, and statistical techniques that Keynes himself did not supply is practically identical to the assessment of the economists concerning Keynes' GT. Again, economists argue that

Keynes had brilliant ideas and intuitions, but that he did not develop them explicitly. Therefore, other researchers had to provide the mathematical modeling that was missing. In the author's view, there is simply no support for these types of bizarre assessments. The reader should note that Kyburg's performance with respect to Keynes' contributions in the 1998-2003 period is no better than his assessment made in 1968 (Bets and Beliefs, A. Phil. Qart., 5, 54-63) or in 1983 (Bets and Beliefs, revised and reprinted in H.E. Kyburg, 1983, Epistemology and Inference, pp. 63-78). Keynes is given credit for partial orders and the two dimensional structure of rational belief [probability (or expectations) and weight (or reliability or confidence)]. Keynes' accomplishments, however, go far beyond what Kyburg acknowledges.

What is clear is that Kyburg, like Ramsey, has not read beyond Chapter 4 (or 6) of the *TP*, skipping those chapters in which Keynes provides his formal analysis. In a striking correspondence, economists rarely read beyond Chapter 3 of the General Theory, since pages 24-30 of Chapter 3 contain the supposed core of Keynes' theory. Of course, the core is in Chapter 20 with an extension in Chapter 21 of the GT (pages 304-306).

The gross ignorance of Keynes' work in the *TP* is exemplified in the work of Runde, Fioretti, and Weatherson (Cambridge J. Of Econ., 2002). The failure of the above individuals to cover Chapters 5, 10, 15, and 17 of the *TP* has led to published work in professional journals which is at best shoddy and shabby. Economists from Ramsey to Stohs to Lawson to Runde to Weatherson love to talk about Keynes' strange, mysterious, unfathomable non-numerical probabilities. All they are doing is displaying their gross ignorance. Keynes presented a fully operational theory of probability that can be applied in the real world.

In this essay, I have shown that the "scholarly" work done on J.M. Keynes by economists, from Weintraub (1975) to Weatherson (2002), on the *TP*, is very poor. Unfortunately, based on the incomplete work by Kyburg, Levi, and Achinstein, the work by philosophers is not much better. It appears that philosophers have just accepted the Ramsey diatribes on faith. Clearly, the 1922 and 1926 "reviews" of Keynes' TP by Ramsey represent the worst two publications of his life.

Footnotes

1   There are a number of other severe errors in Ramsey's essay. I will go over just three of them. Ramsey states:

> "They may . . . say that it is incomparable with any numerical relation, but a relation about which so little can be truly said will be of little scientific use . . ." (Ramsey, p. 28).

and, in a similar vein,

> "But anyone who tries to decide by Mr. Keynes' methods what are the proper alternatives to regard as equally probable in molecular mechanics, e.g., in Gibbs' phase-space, will soon be convinced that it is a matter of physics rather than pure logic" (Ramsey, p. 46).

and finally,

> ". . . the principle of indifference can now be altogether dispensed with . . ." (Ramsey, p. 46).

Ramsey completely ignores Keynes' analysis in Chapter 8 of the *TP*. Keynes states:

> "The generalized frequency theory which I propose to put forward . . . differs from Venn's in several important respects" (Keynes, 1921, p. 101).

This is a major improvement over the various frequency theories extant in 1921, although Keynes recognizes that it has three of the same problems, the reference class problem, the need to use *one* exact precise number to represent the probability estimate of a statistical frequency and the question of relevance. However, Keynes' special theory easily deals with statistical mechanics (Ramsey's "Gibbs phase-space").

But, ". . . the theory of this Treatise is the generalized theory, comprehending within it such applications of the idea of statistical truth-frequency as have validity" (Keynes, 1921, p. 104). Ramsey ignores Keynes' analysis of Chapter 29 where Keynes suggests Tchebycheff's theorem is a sound generalized approach incorporating the normal, binomial, and poisson distributions as special cases that can be used when the special assumptions (strict application of the law of large numbers and central limit theorem guaranteeing the *stability* over time of the frequencies) are shown to hold.

Finally Keynes' support for a heavily qualified use of the principle of indifference (the assumption of a uniform or rectangular probability distribution) gives the correct answer for the probabilities of Boltzmann undistinguishable particles (p= 1/9), for Bose-Einstein distinguishable particles (p= 1/6) and for Dirac-Fermi distinguishable particles (p= 1/3).

Ramsey's two reviews of Keynes in 1922 and 1926, are worthless as far as making a scientific evaluation of Keynes' work in the *TP*. My recommendation is that any reader of the *TP* skip Ramsey's reviews. Ramsey was simply unable to comprehend Keynes' analysis.

2   Garner's confused and error-filled 1983 attempt to "clarify" what Keynes meant in the *TP* by "non-numerical" can be traced back to his earlier 1982 article in JPKE. He commits a number of errors, directly traceable to the fact that, like E. Roy Weintraub and Stohs before him, and Carabelli, O'Donnell, Fitzgibbons, Davis, Runde, Cottrell, Gerrard, and Weatherson after him, Garner's "reading" of the *TP* consists of Chapter 3 and a few other pages selected in a haphazard fashion from a few other chapters. Garner claims the following:

> "Keynes' mature views on uncertainty and decision-making appear in the *General Theory* (1964) and the *Quarterly Journal of Economics* (1937). He described a world of *imperfect* information and *nonrepetitive* events in which probability theory has little validity" (Garner, 1982, p. 413).

Garner must mean "little application". There is no such concept as "has little validity". An approach is either valid or not valid. Garner is just wrong. Keynes, on pages 239-241 of the GT makes it explicit that probability is used is calculating the risk premium and confidence is used in calculating the liquidity premium. Next, Garner claims,

> "Conventional theorists, using probability-based models, have shown that incomplete information can cause Pareto-inefficient equilibria or complete market breakdown (Akerlof, 1970; Spence, 1974; Stiglitz, 1975). However, even these models miss Keynes' basic point, for he believed that the lack of homogeneity rules out *any* application of the probability calculus in cases of uncertainty" (Garner, 1982, p. 414).

This is simply false. The probability calculus is ruled out completely only in cases when w=0, where w is Keynes' index for the weight of the evidence specified in the *TP* (Keynes, 1921, p. 315, Ft. 2). The case of ignorance, or total or complete uncertainty, occurs if w=0. If w>0 but <1, "we have a genuine probability, even when the evidence upon which it is founded is slight" (Keynes, 1921, p. 310). The question of importance, then, is not whether the probability calculus can be applied, but how confident the decision maker is that the probability estimates, either point or interval, are reliable.

Garner next claims that,

> "Shackle and Keynes agreed on the fundamental nature of uncertainty and on the irrelevance of the probability calculus to most major business decisions" (Garner, 1982, p. 416).

Shackle and Keynes, contrary to Garner, do not agree in general. Any agreement is restricted to the case where w=0. Note that Shackle argues, as does his pupil and disciple Paul Davidson, that w=0 or w=1, contrary to Keynes who argues that 0<w<1, as well as w=0 or W=1.

Shackle and Davidson have little or no connection to J.M. Keynes, beyond the fact that like Keynes, they differentiate uncertainty from risk. However, their definition is, in general, opposed by Keynes' definition.

J.T. Harvey (1998) essentially provides an updated (Garner is not cited) version of Garner (1982, 1983), arguing that Tversky-Kahnemans prospect theory can be used to operationalize Keynes' *TP* approach by serving as a foundation of what Harvey calls "Heuristic Judgment Theory" (HJT).

"Both interpretations and forecasts employ the subprocesses that assign, implicitly or explicity, probabilities and confidence levels [Keynes 1920]" (Harvey, 1998, 51).

Harvey overlooks the fact that long before Tversky, Kahneman or Harvey were even born, Keynes, in the *TP*, had provided a fully operational approach to decision making that is superior to Prospect Theory or HJT, as well as demonstrating that Bethamite Utilitarianism (rational choice-expected utility theory) is a special case of his own general theory of decision making specified by Keynes' C coefficient model in Chapter 26 of the *TP*. Harvey adds nothing new to Garner's originally defective argument.

References

Achinstein, P. (2001). The Book of Evidence. Oxford U. Press.

Baddeley, M. (1999). "Keynes on rationality, expectations, and investment". In Keynes, Post-Keynesian in a Political Economy, Vol. III, ed. by C. Sardoni and P. Kriesler. Routledge, pp. 196-213.

Bateman, B. (1995). "The right person, in the right place, at the right time: how mathematical expectations came into macroeconomics". In Measurement, Quantification and Economic Analysis: Numeracy in Economics, ed. by I. Rima. Routledge, pp. 230-244.

_____(1994). "In the Realm of Concept and Circumstance", HOPE, 26, 99-116.

_____(1991). "Das Maynard Keynes Problem", *Cambridge Journal of Economics* 15: 101-11.

_____(1990). "Keynes, induction, and econometrics", HOPE, 22, 359-380.

_____(1988). "G.E. Moore and J.M. Keynes: a missing chapter in the history of the Expected Utility Model", *American Economic Review* 78: 1098-106.

_____(1987). "Keynes' Changing Conception of Probability", *Economics and Philosophy* 3:97-119.

Bateman, B. and Davis, J.B. (eds) (1991). Keynes and Philosophy: Essays on the Origins of Keynes' Thought, Aldershot: Edward Elgar.

Boole, G. (1854). The Laws of Thought. New York: Dover reprint, 1958.

Carabelli, A. (2002). "Keynes on probability, uncertainty and tragic choices". In Competing Economic Theories, ed. by S. Nistico and D. Tosato. Routledge, pp. 249-279.

_____(1998). "Keynes on probability, uncertainty and tragic choices", Cahiers d'Economie Politique 30-1:187-226.

_____(1995). "Uncertainty and measurement in Keynes: probability and organicness." In S. Dow and J. Hillard (eds.) (1995).

_____(1988). On Keynes' Method. London and New York: St. Martin's Press.

Coates, J.M. (1996). The Claims of Common Sense: Moore, Wittgenstein, Keynes and the Social Sciences, Cambridge: Cambridge University Press.

Cottrell, A. (1993). "Keynes' theory of probability and its relevance to his economics: three theses", Economics and Philosophy 9: 25-51.

Davis, J.B. (1994a). Keynes' philosophical thinking. In J.B. Davis (ed.) The state of Interpretation of Keynes, Boston: Kluwer Academic Publishers, pp. 223-44.

Dow, A. and Dow, S. (1985). "Animal spirits and rationality". In T. Lawson and H. Pesaran (eds) (1985).

Dow, S. C. (1995). "Uncertainty about uncertainty." In S.C. Dow and J. Hillard (eds) (1995), pp. 117-27.

Dow, S. C. and Hillard, J. V. (eds.) (1995), Keynes, Knowledge and Uncertainty, Aldershot: Edward Elgar.

Fioretti, G. (1998). John Maynard Keynes and Johannes von Kries, History of Economic Ideas 6:51-80.

_____(2001). Von Kries and the other "German logicians": non-numerical probabilities before Keynes', Economics and Philosophy 17:245-73.

Fitzgibbons, A. (1988). Keynes' Vision: A New Political Economy, Oxford: Oxford University Press.

Garner, A.C. (1982). "Uncertainty, Human Judgement, and Economic Decisions", JPKE, 4, 413-424.

_____(1983). "Comment", HOPE, 15, 83-86. Harvey J.T. (1998). "Heuristic Judgment Theory", JEI, 32, 47-64.

Gerrard, B. (1994). "Beyond rational expectations: a constructive interpretation of Keynes' analysis of behaviour under uncertainty", Economic Journal 104:327-37.

Gillies, D. and Ietto-Gillies, G. (1991). "Intersubjective probabilities and economics", Review of Political Economy 3(4): 393-417.

Hailperin, T. (1965). "Best Possible Inequalities for the Probability of a Logical Function of Events", AMM, 72, 343-359.

_____(1976). Boole's Logic and Probability. Studies in Logic and the Foundations of Mathematics 85. Amsterdam: North Holland.

_____(1984). "Probability Logic", Notre-Dame Journal of Formal Logic, 25, 198-212.

Keynes, J.M. (1921). A Treatise on Probability. London: MacMillan. (1979 AMS Reprint.)

Kyburg, H.E. (2003). SIPTA Newsletter. Vol. I, No. 1 (January). (Reprint of speech given by H. Kyburg at 2001 SIPTA banquet.)

Kyburg, H.E. (1998-2000). Interval-Valued Probabilities. (*http://www.sipta.org*).

Lawson, T. (1987). "The Relative/Absolute Nature of Knowledge and Economic Analysis", Ed, 97, 951-78.

_____(1985). "Uncertainty and economic analysis", Economic Journal 95: 909-27.

Lawson T. and Pesaran, H. (eds) (1985) Keynes' Economics: Methodological Issues, Beckenham: Croom Helm.

McCann, C.R., Jr. (1994). Probability Foundations of Economic Theory, London: Routledge.

Marchionatti, R. (1999). On Keynes' animal spirits, Kyklos 52: 415-39.

Meeks, J. G. T. (1991). Keynes on the rationality of decision procedures under uncertainty: the investment decision. In J.G. T. Meeks (ed.) (1991).

O'Donnell, R. M. (1989). Keynes: Philosophy, Economics and Politics, London: Macmillan.

_____(1991a). Keynes on probability, expectations, and uncertainty. In R.M. O'Donnell (ed.) (1991b), pp. 3-60.

_____(ed.)(1991b). Keynes as Philosopher-Economist, London: Macmillan.

Ramsey, F.P. (1927). "Truth and Probability". In Studies in Subjective Probability, ed. by H. Kyburg, Jr., and H. Smokler. Krieger, (1980), 2nd ed., pp. 25-52.

Regoli, G. (1998-2000). "Comparative Probability Orderings" (Imprecise Probabilities Project: *http://ippserv.rug.ac.be.*)

Runde, J. And Mizuhara, S. (2003). Introduction. In Runde and Mizuhara (eds.) 2003. The Philosophy of Keynes' Economics, p. 8.

Runde, J.H. (1995). Risk, uncertainty and Bayesian decision theory: a Keynesian view. In S.C. Dow and J.V. Hillard (eds) (1995).

_____(1994a). Keynesian uncertainty and liquidity preference, Cambridge Journal of Economics 18: 129-44.

_____(1994b). Keynes after Ramsey: in defence of A Treatise on Probability, Studies in History and Philosophy of Science 25: 97-121.

_____(1994c). The Keynesian probability-relation: in search of a substitute. In J. B. Davis (ed.) The State of Interpretation of Keynes, Boston: Kluwer Academic Publishers, pp. 245-51.

_____(1991). Keynesian uncertainty and the instability of beliefs, Review of Political Economy 3: 125-45.

_____(1990). Keynesian uncertainty and the weight of arguments, Economics and Philosophy 6: 275-92.

Smithson, M.J. (1997-2000). "Human Judgment and Imprecise Probabilities". (Imprecise Probabilities Project: *http://ippserv.rug.ac.be).*

Stohs, M. (1980). "Uncertainty in Keynes' General Theory", HOPE, 12, 372-82.

Walley, P. (1997-1998). "Coherent Upper and Lower Provisions". (Imprecise Probabilities Project: *http://ensmain.rug.ac.be/ipp.)*

_____(1997-2000). "Imprecise Probabilities". (Imprecise Probabilities Project: *http://ippserv.rug.ac.be)*

Weatherson, B. (2002). Keynes, uncertainty and interest rates, Cambridge Journal of Economics 26: 47-62.

Weintraub, E.R. (1975). "Uncertainty and the Keynesian Revolution", HOPE, 7, 530-548.

Winslow, E.G. (1995). Uncertainty and liquidity-preference. In S.C. Dow and J. V. Hillard (eds) (1995).

_____(1989). Organic interdependence, uncertainty and economic analysis, Economic Journal 99: 1173-82.

_____(1986a). Human logic and Keynes' economics', Eastern Economic Journal 12:413-30.

5

How Issac Levi Gambled with the Truth and Lost Badly: Why philosophy and economics fail to satisfy the necessary "transparency" condition to be considered scientific

Abstract— In Chapter IX of Levi's *Gambling With Truth* (1967), at least 10 errors of omission or commission were committed. These errors were then passed down over the next 36 years to a number of other researchers, who then passed them down to others. A necessary condition for a field to be considered scientific is that it be transparent—"that no result is accepted unless and until it is checked (and re-checked) by someone else".[1] A scientific field is one where errors are corrected *within* the discipline. This paper demonstrates that, in philosophy and economics, results are not checked and rechecked for reliability and accuracy, nor is there any error correcting mechanism present.

1. Introduction

The paper is presented in the following way. Section I and II deal with J.M. Keynes. First, it is shown that J.M. Keynes provided an index for weight of evidence. Second, Keynes provided a decision rule incorporating this index for weight of evidence. Third, Keynes provided a full analysis of this decision rule. Fourth, ignorance, uncertainty (lack of weight) and risk are all differentiated in his presentation in Chapter 26 of the *Treatise on Probability* (TP). Finally, it is noted that in the history of decision theory or science, J.M. Keynes stands alone in being the *first* to provide such an index as well as a clear cut, specific decision rule with clear cut specific analytic results. The remaining sections show the errors of I. Levi and how they have been passed down into the philosophical and economics literature. No error-correction process is apparent in these fields. Thus, those fields are not scientific since errors are not only not removed, but passed down to others.

2. Keynes, his Index of Weight of Evidence, and his conventional coefficient of risk and weight.

In Chapter 6 of the TP, Keynes states:

> "The conclusion, that the 'weight' and the 'probability' of an argument are independent properties, may possibly introduce a difficulty into the discussion of the application of probability to practice.[1] For in deciding on a course of action, it seems plausible to suppose that we ought to take account of the weight as well as the probability of different expectations. But it is difficult to think of any clear example of this, and I do not feel sure that the theory of 'evidential weight' has much practical significance.—[1]See also Chapter XXXVL. § 7."

In Sections 7 and 8 of Chapter 26 of the TP, we find the following extension of his argument from Chapter 6 of the TP:

> "There seems, at any rate, a good deal to be said for the conclusion that, other things being equal, that course of action is preferable which involves least risk and about the results of which we have the most complete knowledge. In marginal cases, therefore, the coefficients of weight and risk

as well as that of probability are relevant to our conclusion. It seems natural to suppose that they should exert some influence in other cases also, the only difficulty in this being the lack of any principle for the calculation of the degree of their influence. A high weight and the absence of risk increase *pro tanto* the desirability of the action to which they refer, but we cannot measure the amount of the increase.

•

•

•

We could, if we liked, define a conventional coefficient c of weight and risk, such as $c=2pw/(1+q)(1+w)$, where w measures the 'weight', which is equal to unity when p=1 and w=1, and to zero when p=0 or w=0, and has an intermediate value in other cases.[2-2]If $pA=p'A'$, $w>w'$, and $q=q'$, then $cA>c'A'$; if $pA=p'A'$, $w=w'$, and $q<q'$, then $cA>c'A'$; if $pA=p'A'$, $w>w'$, and $q<q'$, then $cA>c'A'$; but if $pA=p'A'$, $w>w'$, and $q>q'$, we cannot in general compare cA and c'A'"(Keynes, 1921, p. 315; 1973, p. 347).

Keynes diferentiates between "very uncertain", "greatly uncertain", "ignorance" and "even when the evidence . . . is slight" on page 310 of the TP. (The same wording shows up in Chapter 12 of Keynes' General Theory.) Risk is discussed on page 315 and page 355 of Chapter 29 of the TP, which follows from Keynes' comment on page 314 of the TP.

Keynes has defined an index for measuring weight of evidence on the unit interval [0, 1], where w=weight of evidence. Thus, $w\varepsilon[0,1]$.

A w of zero corresponds to ignorance. A low w corresponds to "greatly uncertain", "very uncertain, or "even when the evidence . . . . is slight". Risk corresponds to a w of 1. Risk can be linear or non-linear in terms of preference or can be represented by a normal probability distribution if symmetric or a skewed distribution if non-symmetric. Thus,

0 less than or equal to w less than or equal to 1.

This index was formed by Keynes in the same way that probability was defined on the unit interval [0, 1]:

0 less than or equal to p less than or equal to 1, or pE[0,1], where p stands for "probability".

The standard way of constructing such indices is a job for a sixth grade grammar school student.

Given p+q=1, the probabilities are

0 less than or equal to p/p+q less than or equal to 1

and

0 less than or equal to q/q+p less than or equal to 1,

where p is now the probability of success and q the probability of failure. If p=1, q=0 and if q=1, p=0. The "intermediate cases" are between 0 and 1.

The w index is identical in its construction format. Define K= relevant knowledge and I= relevant ignorance.

Given K+I=1, the weights are

0 less than or equal to K/K+I less than or equal to 1

and

0 less than or equal to I/K+I less than or equal to 1, where w=K/K+I.

If K=1, I=0 and w=1. If I=1, K=0 and w=0. The intermediate cases are between 0 and 1. Keynes has provided a complete mathematical definition of ignorance (w=0), uncertainty (w between 0 and 1) and risk (w=1). One can use the verbiage "total uncertainty" or "complete uncertainty" or "we simply do not know". However, these phrases all translate as w=0 in Keynes' index of weight, w.

Keynes, in his footnote 2, provides a decision rule that solves all the paradoxes and anomalies that have been published (in academic philosophy, psychology, and economics journals) since World War II.

3. The Errors in I. Levi's Chapter IX of *Gambling With Truth*.

Levi starts his Chapter IX by making a number of claims.

Claim one—

"1] An Alleged Paradox.

Consider an urn that contains 10 balls, of which an unknown percentage are black and the remainder white. A sample with replacement, consisting of 101 draws, is to be made from the urn. The question arises: what is the probability that on the 101st draw a black ball will be obtained (a) relative to the evidence available prior to the first 100 draws, and (b) when the first 100 draws have been made and close to 50 percent have shown black?

The answer to both questions is that the probability to be assigned to the sentence "On the 101st trial, a black ball will be drawn" is .5.

John Maynard Keynes, who devoted some attention to the notion of "weight of arguments", insisted upon making a distinction between weight and probability. However, he did not seem to think that differing situations of type (a) and type (b) necessitated the use of an index of weight of evidence" (Levi, pp. 139-140).

Claim two—

"The conclusion, that the 'weight' and the 'probability' of an argument are independent properties, may possibly introduce a difficulty into the discussion of the application of probability to practice. For in deciding on a course of action, it seems plausible to suppose that we ought to take account of the weight as well as the probability of different expectations. But it is difficult to think of any clear example of this, and I do not feel sure that the theory of 'evidential weight' has much practical significance.[3]

Keynes' failure to think of a clear example in which weight of evidence plays a role in practical applications cannot be attributed to lack of sufficient imagination to be able to envisage illustrations of the sort introducted by Peirce and later by Popper. He does, in point of fact, use urn examples in discussing weight. But instead of introducing these examples as puzzles that necessitate the introduction of a notion of weight of evidence for their solution, he takes for granted the distinction between weight and probability, and uses the urn models to illustrate how weight of evidence can, on some occasions, be measured by the probable error in estimates of the long-run frequencies that result from large-scale sampling with replacement.[4]" (Levi, p. 140).

Claim 3—

"Quite aside from the eminence of Keynes' authority, it is rather difficult to see how the urn example, and others like it, raise any serious problems" (Levi, p. 141).

Claim 4—

"2] Amounts of Evidence.

According to Keynes, probability measures the "balance" between favorable and unfavorable evidence. Weight of argument or weight of evidence is a "balance, not between the favorable and the unfavorable evidence, but between *absolute* amounts of relevant knowledge and relevant ignorance, respectively."[5] Keynes makes clear in his discussion that by "knowledge" he means the totality of information accepted as evidence. A measure of weight of evidence becomes, for him, a measure of the amount of relevant evidence.

Keynes explicitly mentions his difficulties in finding any important application for the notion of weight of evidence. He does, however, cite one context in which it might be useful.

We may argue that, when our knowledge is slight but capable of increase, the course of action, which will, relative to such knowledge, probably produce the greatest amount of good, will often consist in the acquisition of more knowledge. But there clearly comes a point when it is no longer worth while to spend trouble, before acting, in the acquisition of further information, and there is no evident principle by which to determine *how far we* ought to carry our maxim of strengthening the weight of our argument. A little reflection will probably convince the reader that this is a very confusing problem.[6]" (Levi, p. 141).

Claim 5—

"Keynes takes note of the obvious fact that on some occasions a decision-maker will defer action until further evidence is in. On the other hand, he will sometimes judge additional evidence collection to be pointless. Keynes raises the question: "How much evidence is enough evidence?" He equates this with the question: "How great must the weight of evidence be before further evidence collection becomes pointless?"

If the notion of weight of evidence has any significance in inductive inference, it seems most likely that its importance is to be found in connection with this "confusing" problem. Note, however, that Keynes has made one tacit assumption here, which ought to be scrutinized. He asks *how much* evidence is enough evidence. This presupposes that sufficiency of evidence is a function of absolute amounts of relevant evidence.

Sometimes, however, an increase in the amount of relevant evidence will decrease its sufficiency. A physician might want to find out whether Mr. X has disease D or E, which call for difference therapies. Relative to the evidence available to him, he feels justified in diagnosing D. Subsequently, new evidence is obtained that casts doubt on that diagnosis, but without being decisive in favor of E. The amount of relevant evidence has increased; but would it not be plausible to say that the need for new evidence increased after the increase of relevant evidence?

Considerations such as this suggest that it is preferable to view weight of evidence not as a measure of the absolute amount of relevant evidence, but as an index of the sufficiency of available evidence. Weight of evidence would then be viewed as of high value when no further evidence is needed and would fall away from that high value as the demand for new evidence increases.

The problem still remains of determining the conditions under which new evidence is needed and when it is pointless; this remains, as Keynes says, a confusing problem. But some partial headway might be made by avoiding Keynes' question-begging assumption that the issue is one of absolute amounts of relevant evidence" (Levi, p. 142).

Claim 6—

"The investigator has a decision problem in which he has two options: to remain with the status quo or to follow the evidence-collecting policy.[7]"

"[7]Some writers (for example, A. Wald, *statistical Decision Functions* [New York: Wiley, 1950], Chapter 1) suggest that a decision to collect evidence can be viewed as a decision to suspend judgment. This does not seem plausible in connection with cognitive decision problems. The reaching of conclusions is not *deferred* until new evidence is obtained. Rather, new evidence is obtained in order to reach stronger conclusions; or (in the case of the nonskeptic), to check conclusions already obtained. In practical decision-making, it is undoubtedly true that action is deferred until new evidence is obtained; but in the case of belief, commitments made relative to given evidence can always be revised in the light of new evidence" (Levi, p. 144).

Claim 7—

"6] Conclusion.

The aim of this chapter has been to indicate one way in which degrees of confidence are important to inductive inference. It has been suggested that the need for new evidence is a decreasing function of the degree of confidence with which the available evidence warrants accepting the strongest sentence justifiably accepted on that evidence. The few details of an account of weight of evidence (understood as an index of the need for new evidence) that have been offered here are neither complete nor immune from further criticism. Hopefully, however, enough has been said to suggest the presence of an important network of questions and the relevance of degrees of confidence to these questions" (Levi, p. 152).

Levi's claim 1 is false. His "alleged paradox" is in fact a slightly different version of the two color-two urn Ellsberg Paradox. It is also false to claim that Keynes "did not seem to think that differing situations of type (a) and type (b) necessitated the use of an index of weight of evidence". Keynes provided such an index and a *general* solution to *all* Ellsberg type problems on page 315 of his TP in footnote 2. See discussion above in Section II.

Levi's claim 2 is false. In the quotation from Chapter 6, page 76 of the TP, Levi leaves out footnote 1 from line 3 that appears after "to practice". In this footnote, Keynes directs the reader to Chapter 26, Section 7. In Section 8, a continuation of Section 7, the reader will find Keynes' analysis. Levi's claim about Keynes' failure to think of a clear example of practical application . . ." is also false. Keynes applies his analysis to ethical-moral decision-making. Levi's further statement, that Keynes "takes for granted the distinction between weight and probability" and does not introduce the notion of weight of evidence as necessary for their solution is the result of Levi's earlier failure to study Chapter 26, Sections 7 and 8, of the TP.

Levi's claim 3 is false. Keynes does not rely on his authority. He creates an index of weight of evidence and incorporates it in his decision rule c. He then provides *general* solutions for *all* the paradoxes discussed in Post WWII decision theory. Most of these paradoxes are due to the failure to include a weight or support of evidence index.

Levis's claim 4 is false. Again, it ignores the index of weight of evidence, o≤w≤1, created by Keynes on page 315 of the TP.

Levi's claim 5 is false. It is simply nonsense to claim that "by avoiding Keynes' question-begging assumption that the issue is one of absolute amounts of relevant evidence" one can come "to view weight of evidence not as a measure of the absolute amount of relevant evidence, but as an index of the sufficiency of available evidence". Keynes already did this 9-20 years before Levi was born. Nowhere in the TP does Keynes present "a measure of the absolute amount of relevant evidence". Keynes presents

o less than or equal to w less than or equal to 1.

Of course, Keynes also deals with comparing *different* w's. Assume w′>w. Then the absolute amount of relevant evidence supporting w′ is greater than the absolute amount of relevant evidence supporting w. w′ is the weight of evidence of type (b). w is the weight of evidence of type (a). Obviously, w′>w.

Levi's claim 6 is false. It is not true in the case of investing in long lived physical durable capital goods (factories, machines) or in new innovations involving economies of scale that "... in the case of belief, commitments made relative to given evidence can always be revised in the light of new evidence". Such investments are irreversible, irrevocable, or "cast in concrete". Keynes discussed the application of his concept of weight of evidence (i.e., "confidence") to investment theory and the holding of money (his liquidity preference theory) in Chapters 12 and 13 of the General Theory (Keynes, 1936, GT). It is obvious that Levi is completely unaware of Keynes' 1936 extensions of his theory of evidential weight to economics in the GT.

Levi's claim 7 is false. Keynes had already developed an index to measure weight of evidence and had integrated it into his decision coefficient c non linearly.

The conclusion reached is that Chapter IX of Levi's *Gambling With Truth* should be completely rewritten in a future edition or withdrawn. It will be shown that this work is the foundation for a continuing series of errors that appear in the economics and philosophy literature from 1985-2002.

4. The Errors of Lawson

Lawson (1985, pp. 913-914) claims that Keynes did not define uncertainty in the TP. This is the same as Levi's claim that Keynes did not specify an index of weight of evidence in the TP. Like Levi's claim, Lawson's claim is false. Keynes defines ignorance, uncertainty, and risk on page 315 of the TP (1921, p. 315). If w=0, the condition is one of ignorance or total uncertainty. If o<w<1, the condition is one of uncertainty or partial ignorance. If w=1, the condition is one of risk.

In Lawson (1987, p. 953), the same errors are repeated: Lawson states:

"Depending upon what 'completeness of information' means here . . ." (Lawson 1987, p. 953).

He then makes the Bayesian error of confusing imprecise probabilities with weight of evidence (uncertainty) problems that result in indeterminate probabilities:

> . . . Keynes . . . distinguishes three types of probability-relation: the first, where a probability-relation is numerically indeterminate and possibly not even comparable to . . . other probability relations . . . the first type of probability, for Keynes, corresponds to a situation of *uncertainty* (see Lawson, 1985) . . ." (Lawson, 1987, p. 953).

Keynes had already refuted Lawson back in 1921, since "weight cannot, then, be explained in terms of probability . . . . The conclusion, that the 'weight' and the 'probability' of an argument are independent properties . . ." (Keynes, 1921, p. 76).

Obviously, uncertainty = partial ignorance = an intermediate degree of weight of evidence can't possibly be related to the question of the *form* a probability estimate takes [point, interval, ranking (ordinal)] on.

5. The errors of Runde

Runde combines the errors of Levi and Lawson. Runde confuses Keynes' logical symbol V, meaning "weight of the argument", with Keynes' mathematical treatment of weight, which uses w, where w means "weight of the evidence", in Chapter 26. The logical symbol V is used by Keynes in the following manner: $V(a\acute{a}hh_1) > V(a\acute{a}h)$, unless h_1 is irrelevant and where h and h_1 represent *single units* of information. V is a part of Keynes' symbolic (formal) logic exposition. Runde strangely uses $V(x\acute{a}h)$ and not Keynes' $V(a\acute{a}h)$. Runde states,

> "A somewhat different conception of weight appears at the beginning of Chapter 6 of the *Treatise*, where weight is described as the *balance* of the absolute amounts of relevant

knowledge and relevant ignorance on which a probability is based:

> The magnitude of the probability of an argument . . . depends upon a balance between what may be termed the favourable and the unfavourable evidence; a new piece of evidence which leaves the balance unchanged, also leaves the probability of the argument unchanged. But it seems that there may be another respect in which some kind of quantitative comparison between arguments is possible. This comparison turns upon a balance, not between the favourable and the unfavourable evidence, but between the *absolute* amounts of relevant knowledge and of relevant ignorance respectively. (CW VIII, p. 77).

> If relevant knowledge and relevant ignorance are represented by K, and I, then weight might be represented as $V(x/h) = K_r/I_r$." (Runde, 1990, p. 280).

Of course, Keynes' "quantitative comparison" . . . "between the absolute amounts of relevant knowledge and of relevant ignorance" takes place in Chapter 26 of the TP on page 315 *after* Keynes has normalized weight on the unit interval [0, 1].

Of course, it is impossible that Keynes, a world class applied mathematician, would set

$$V(aáh) = K_r/I_r$$

since every third grade student knows you can't divide by 0. In the case of certainty of evidence, $I_t=0$, $K_t=1$, but 1/0 is undefined in arithmetic. Runde continues in his error-filled ways as he makes his way to Chapter 26 of the TP and analyzes Keynes' term "degree of completeness of the information".

> "For present purposes, however, the important phrase is Keynes' reference to the "degree of completeness of the

information" on which the probability is based, a phrase he repeats two pages further on. If "knowledge" and "information" (and "evidence") are taken as synonymous terms as Keynes appears to do, the degree of completeness of the information on which a probability is based might be expressed as follows:

$$V(x/h) = K_t/(K_t + I_t) \qquad (3)$$

which reduces to:

$$1/(w+1) \qquad (4)$$

where $w = I_t/K_t$.

Equation (4) clearly moves in the same way as (2). Accordingly, we may restrict our attention to one of either (2) or (3). Since (3) has more intuitive appeal, I shall henceforth take the second notion of weight (weight$_2$) to be "the degree of completeness of the information on which a probability is based" (Runde, p. 281).

Again, $w = I_t/K_t$ is mathematically impossible. If one has no relevant information, $K_r = 0$ and $I_r = 1$. However, $I_t/K_t = 1/0$ is undefined.

Runde's penchant for dividing by 0 is strange. Even more so is his foolish attempt to claim that these types of grammar school errors could possibly represent Keynes' ideas on the subject. Only William Johnson, a contemporary of Keynes, comes up with a very similar concept, degree of worth = w.

Runde, by chance, arrives at Keynes' w of Chapter 26. It is

0 less than or equal to w less than or equal to 1

and

0 less than or equal to $K_r/K_r + I_r$ less than or equal to 1.

Again, I repeat that it is mathematically impossible for

$$V(\text{aáh}) = K_r/K_r + I_r,$$

since h can represent only *one* unit of information. Runde confuses V, a logical operator, with w, a mathematical variable. Runde then repeats the entire false analysis of Levi (see Claim 5—Levi, 1968, p. 142).

> "At this stage it is useful to compare weight$_1$ and weight$_2$. In terms of weight$_1$, new evidence "will sometimes decrease the probability of an argument, but it will always increase its weight" (CW VIII, p. 77). The surprising feature of weight$_2$ is that the same conclusion need not follow. New evidence, in other words, may lead to a *decrease* in weight. To see this, it will be helpful to refer again to (3); If I$_r$ does not increase by more than K$_r$, it is clear that weight$_2$ will increase with every increase in K$_r$. But it is surely possible, in principle, that we may sometimes learn something that leads us to drastically reassess I$_r$, to revise it upward by more than any increase in K$_r$. In this case, the accretion of evidence will lead to a *decrease* in weight.
>
> The possibility that weight may decrease with the acquisition of more evidence does not appear in the *Treatise*; indeed, it contradicts many of Keynes' other statements. Nevertheless, a hint of the idea appears in Keynes' remarks that "we may say that the weight is increased when the number of alternatives is reduced, although the ratio of the number of favorable to the number of unfavorable alternatives may not have been disturbed" and ". . . we may say that the weight of the probability is increased, as the field of possibility is contracted" (CW VIII, p. 84). Presumabley, in both of these cases, there is new evidence to suggest that "the number of alternatives is reduced" or that "the field of possibility is contracted." These examples seem to bear the consequence that if new evidence is acquired to the effect that there are more alternatives or a larger field of

possibility than previously imagined, then weight can fall despite our knowledge increasing. In other words, we may have enlarged our perception of relevant ignorance, which suggests that weight would then fall with the acquisition of that evidence." (Runde, 1990, pp. 282-283).

This is nonsense. Given w$\in$[0,1], where w=K/K+I, w will automatically decrease if new evidence increases I. Likewise, it contradicts *none* of Keynes' statements.

All of the errors in Runde (1990) reappear again in Runde (1991):

"When discussing the *nature* of weight, however, Keynes appears to have in mind something more than a mere measure of the absolute amounts of relevant evidence on which probabilities are based. At the beginning of the chapter on weight he describes it as 'a balance . . . between the *absolute* amounts of relevant knowledge and of relevant ignorance respectively, on which a probability is based (CW VIII: 77). And towards the end of the book he refers to weight as 'the degree of completeness of the information upon which a probability is based' (CW VIII, 345). Both of these ideas depend, in part, on the notion of 'relevant ignorance'. Keynes does not discuss this idea at any length, but seems to have something of the following in mind: that relevant ignorance is some measure of our apprehension of the extent of our ignorance about evidence which we know to be relevant to some conclusion. For example, we may know that the price of copper ten years hence has a direct bearing on the prospective yield of an investment, but have no idea of what the price will be at that time. The greater our relevant ignorance, or alternatively, the more incomplete our knowledge relevant to some conclusion, the lower the weight of evidence" (Runde, 1991, p. 132).

Contrary to Runde, by definition of w$\in$[0,1], Keynes has covered the idea of relevant ignorance.

6. The errors of Cottrell (1993)

Cottrell's first error is his claim that "my second thesis . . . is that there is a particular "internal" problem for Keynes in the nexus between his logical theory of probability and the concept of "weight of argument" (Cottrell, p. 26).

There is no "nexus", link or connection between the two. Weight and probability are completely independent. Keynes states this over and over again in Chapter 6 of the TP:

> ". . . the weighing of the amount of evidence is quite a separate process from the *balancing* of the evidence for and against" (Keynes, p. 74).
> "Weight cannot, then, be explained in terms of probability" (Keynes, 1921, p. 76).
> "The conclusion, that the 'weight' and the 'probability' of an argument are independent properties . . ." (Keynes, 1921, p. 76).
> "The weight . . . measures the *sum* of the favourable and unfavourable evidence, the probability measures the *difference*" (Keynes, 1921, p. 77).

Cottrell's second error occurs throughout pages 30-35 as he, following Ramsey, conflates degree of belief with degree of confidence. Keynes' degree of confidence is directly related to $wE[0,1]$. Ramsey has no such measure because Ramsey stupidly confused degree of belief with degree of confidence. Cottrell apes Ramsey.

Cottrell's error is to claim that "while he seems to want to give" weight "a role, his general theory will not allow this" (Cottrell, p. 36). This is intellectual garbage. Keynes' general theory of decision making is presented explicitly on page 315 of the TP. First, Keynes specifies an index of weight of evidence, w, where $wE[0,1]$. Second, Keynes presents his conventional coefficient of risk and weight, c. Third, Keynes works out all possible cases of the application of his c coefficient in an extensive footnote.

The coefficient solves *all* the paradoxes and anomalies of post WWII SEU Theory, including the Allais paradox and all its variants, like the common consequence, ratio or "fanning out" effect, the Ellsberg-Fellner Paradox, the Popper Paradox, the certainty, reflection, isolation and translation effects, the Kunreuther paradox and preference reversal phenomenon. Cottrell's fourth error is his ignorance of the Ellsberg Paradox. Outside of the two error-filled papers of Runde cited by Cottrell, there is no mention of the vast literature surrounding the Ellsberg Paradox. Of course, Ellsberg's first example, the two color urn problem, is identical to Keynes' Chapter 6 example in the TP that is later solved in both Chapters 26 and 30 of the TP. Cottrell's fifth error is to build on an example of A. Ayer, who also overlooked the Ellsberg paradox.

Cottrell bases his faulty analysis on the faulty analysis of Ayer. Ayer discussed two forecasts of an upcoming football match between two teams. Forecast I is based on the teams' *current* form. This would include a *number* of recent games played. Forecast II is based only on a *single* piece of evidence—what happened in the *last* meeting between the two teams. Forecast I is equivalent to Ellsberg's Urn I in the two color problem, while Forecast II is equivalent to Urn II in the Ellsberg two color problem. Cottrell claims that he is going to "examine Keynes' treatment of the issue" (Cottrell, p. 37). However, this does not happen anywhere in the paper.

Cottrell's sixth error is his failure to recognize that $P(a/x_1x_2)$ and $P(a/x_1x_2x_3)$ are *different* probabilities. He quotes Ayer's page 57 mistake verbatim, which requires that a decision be a function of probabilty assessment *alone*. For Keynes, and all logical probability theorists, a decision is a function of *both* probability *and* weight. So it is also for Ellsberg with his $ index.

Cottrell's seventh error is to use L.J. Cohen's article (Cohen, 1986, p. 266) to support his own. Cohen completely missed Keynes' technical analysis on page 315 of the TP as well as its extension in Chapter 30 of the TP.

Cottrell's eighth error is to base his paper's discussion of weight on the error filled papers of Runde (1990, 1991). (See Cottrell, 1993, p. 41, 48).

Cottrell's ninth error is to conflate risk with uncertainty. The "degree of uncertainty" has nothing to do with "the standard deviation of the individual's probability distribution" (Cottrell, p. 48). Knowledge of a single probability distribution that alone is relevant requires a w=1.

There are an additional four errors in Cottrell's paper. I think that we have covered enough. This is the same Allin Cottrell who proclaimed that Keynes wrote the GT using only N and N_2 variables. Cottrell's claim, that Keynes did not use N_1 nor need N_1, is a mistake that a fourth grade grammar school student would not make. It simply means that Cottrell does not know what the summation sign means mathematically or how it is used in scientific discourse. Of course, the only major change between the 1934 draft copy of the GT and the GT itself is that Keynes introduces summation notation and subscripts (or the suffix r) as part of his attempt to simplify the mathematical notation used in the GT in 1936.

7. The errors of Dow

Dow builds directly on Runde and Lawson:

> "Unfortunately, Keynes did not present an explicit definition of uncertainty" (Dow, 1994, p. 436).

Keynes couldn't have been any more explicit. See Section II above.

Dow states:

> "But as Runde (1990) has pointed out, new evidence might change the assessment of the extent of evidence which would be relevant to the proposition. Weight might thus decline if new evidence more fully revealed the extent of relevant ignorance. This insight pinpoints the importance of focusing on the process of generating knowledge of what is relevant. It implies that ignorance is no more absolute a benchmark than knowledge, since

understanding of ignorance itself requires knowledge. This line of reasoning suggests that uncertainty may best be understood in terms of first-order and second-order uncertainty.

.

.

.

Second order uncertainty refers to the degree of uncertainty attached to propositions about the nature and extent of evidence which would be relevant; i.e. to the degree of uncertainty attached to assessing weight. (In principle, this classification could proceed to ever-higher orders.) Put another way, second-order uncertainty is uncertainty about uncertainty" (Dow, 1994, p. 437).

Dow has simply made a logical error. There is no such thing as uncertainty about uncertainty. This is simply a logical infinite regress, since one must then ponder third-order uncertainty, i.e., uncertainty about uncertainty about uncertainty, ad infinatum. She then repeats, in a later paper, the Levi error, repeated by Runde:

> "Keynes used weight both as an absolute and a relative concept. According to the former, weight is measured by the absolute amount of relevant evidence. But the latter introduces the notion of relevant ignorance. After referring to probability as depending on the balance of favourable and unfavorable evidence, Keynes introduces the concept of weight as an additional respect in which arguments may be compared:

>> This comparison turns on a balance, not between the favourable and the unfavourable evidence, but between the *absolute* amounts of relevant knowledge and of relevant ignorance respectively. (TP; 77)

> The introduction of the notion of relevant ignorance opens up possibilities for further refinements. Runde's

(1990b) addition to Keynes' notion of weight is particularly
suggestive. He points out that increased evidence, rather
than increasing weight, may reduce weight if it reveals new
realms of ignorance. In particular, new evidence may reveal
that what was understood to be the best model is in fact
inadequate" (Dow, 1995, p. 120).

This leads Dow to publish the best example of a logical infinite
regress argument that this author has ever seen. In her Table 7.1,
U stands for uncertainty. Supposedly, Uñ stands for infinite
uncertainty about uncertainty:

Table 7.1 A taxonomy of uncertainty

	p measurable (K=1)	p not measurable (K<1)
U_1	sigma (epsilon)—	
U_2	1-p	low order of p
U_{3a}	$1/w_1$	$1/w_1$
U_{3b}	—	$1-w_2$
U_{4a}	—	low order of K
U_{4b}	—	low order of K relat. to I
:	:	:
U infinity—		K=0, I=1

p=a/h
w_1 = h/K
w_2 = (h/h+i)/K
K=K[R (h,i)]/h
I=I[R (h,i)]/h
Where:
p = probability
a = argument
h = evidence
I = ignorance of evidence
R = relevance
K = knowledge of R, 0<K less than or equal to 1
I = ignorance of R, 0 less than or equal to I<1
w = weight of evidence

Compare this intellectual quagmire with what Keynes actually did accomplish in this area:

0 less than or equal to w less than or equal to 1

Keynes' index is simple, straight forward, general, and easy to use in practice. Dow is simply confused.

8. The error of L.J. Cohen

Cohen, in his otherwise excellent 1986 BJPS article, indirectly contributed to the misinterpretation of Keynes, concerning weight of evidence, in his Section 2, titled inappropriately, "Why did Keynes Not Appreciate How Weight Matters?".

Cohen has simply overlooked Chapter 26 of the TP. In fact, nowhere in Cohen's collected body of published work has he ever dealt with all the advances made by Keynes. Keynes had hard analysis and not just "his various intuitions", "these intuitions", "intuitive idea", etc. (Cohen, 1986, p. 267).

9. The errors of Weatherson

All the previous errors are now incorporated in the paper by Weatherson. First, Weatherson confuses imprecise probabilities with indeterminate probabilities. Although *both* are interval estimates, that is the only similarity. To his great credit, Levi has shown the fallacies of the Bayesian imprecise probabilities literature in Levi, 1974 and Levi, 1985. Keynes' interval estimates, i.e., his "non numerical" probabilities which translates as "not by a single numeral", are indeterminate. Keynes deals with the imprecision problem in Chapters 29 and 30 of the TP, in his discussion of estimates derived using the normal probability distribution vs. the more imprecise estimates using Chebyshev's Inequality.

Second, Weatherson claims:

"2. Keynes and imprecise probabilities. Obviously enough, this is not the theory that Keynes formally endorses, either in his *Treatise on Probability* or in his economic writings. Nevertheless, I think it is an important theory for understanding Keynes' use of uncertainty. This is because it, and it alone, captures all of the underlying motivations of Keynes' theory of uncertainty. Hence any economic consequences of uncertainty Keynes wants to draw will have to be derivable from this theory. I have so far spoken blithely of 'Keynes' theory of uncertainty', implicitly assuming there is such a unique theory. In recent years, a number of authors (e.g., Runde, 1994A; Davis, 1994; Coates, 1996; Bateman, 1996) have questioned this assumption, saying that Keynes changed his theory between the writing of the *Treatise on Probability* and *The General Theory*." (Weatherson, 2002, p. 50).

This is simply false, as Weatherson admits. Weatherson can find Keynes' theory of uncertainty in Chapter 26 of the TP, Sections 7 and 8.

Third, Weatherson claims:

"Keynes avoids this implausibililty by tightening up the definition of irrelevance. He says that e is irrelevant to p/q iff there are no propositions e_1 & e_2 such that e is logically equivalent to e_1 & e_2 and either e_1 or e_2 is relevant to p/q. Unfortunately, as I noted in the previous paragraph, for virtually any such evidence proposition there will be such propositions e_1 and e_2. This was first noticed by Carnap (1950). Keynes, had he noticed this, would have had three options. He could have conceded that everything is relevant to everything, including last night's baseball results to the identity of Kennedy's assassin; he could have conceded that the order in which evidence appears does matter, or he could have given up the claim that new relevant evidence *always* increases the weight of arguments.

The last option is plausible. Runde (1990) defends it, but for quite different reasons. He thinks weight measures the ratio of evidence we have to total evidence we believe is available. Since new evidence might lead us to believe there is much more evidence available than we had previously suspected, the weight might go down. I believe it holds for a quite different reason, one borne out by Keynes' use of uncertainty in his economics." (Weatherson, 2002, p. 52).

This is false. Weatherson can find his errors corrected for him in Chapter 26 of the TP.

Fourth, Weatherson claims

"Keynes' theory of probability is based around some non-numerical values whose nature and behaviour are left largely unexplained, and a concept of weight which is subject to a telling and simple objection. Nevertheless, his core ideas, that probabilities can but need not be precise, and that we need a concept such as weight as well as just probability, both seem right for more general reasons. Hence the theory here, which captures the Keynesian intuitions while explaining away his mysterious non-numerical values and making the concept of weight more rigorous, looks to be as good as it gets for a Keynesian theory of uncertainty." (Weatherson, 2002, p. 53).

Everything stated here is false. Keynes fully developed his interval estimate technique in Chapters 16 and 18 of the TP. His discussion of "non-numerical probabilities" is illustrated fully on page 39 of the TP. The "non-numerical probabilities" contained in this diagram are in fact intervals since they require *two numbers*, not one, to specify the probability relation. There is no such thing as Weatherson's "mysterious non-numerical values".

Fifth, Weatherson creates his own "conventional coefficient", which is inferior to Keynes' own analysis:

"So let the expected value of investing a certain sum be [alpha, beta], and the expected value of buying a debt with that money be x. Then the agent will invest iff (1-rho) alpha + rho beta greater than or equal to psi, where rho E[0, 1] measures the 'state of confidence'.[2] Now when a crisis erupts, rho will go to 0, and investment will dry up. In such cases, the decision theory is similar to the one advanced by Levi (1980), Strat (1990) and Jaffray (1994). Since we are interested in a theory of unemployment, we are primarily interested in the cases where $ is quite low, in which cases we can say uncertainty is reducing investment." (Weatherson, 2002, p. 54).

Sixth, the extension Weatherson makes to Keynes' Investment Theory concern for confidence is also inferior to Keynes' conventional coefficient. Weatherson claims:

"The most charitable reading of Keynes here is to say he agreed, in principle, with what is sometimes referred to as a Horwitz-style decision rule. If the expected return of an investment is vague over [_, _] then its 'value' is given by (1-rho) alpha + rho beta, where $E[0, 1] is a measure of confidence. By the 1937 article, he has become more interested in the special case where confidence has collapsed and $ is approaching 0. This interpretation would explain all his references to decision making under uncertainty in *The General Theory* and subsequent discussion, provided we make the safe assumption that 'cold calculation' would only have us spend x on an investment with expected return [alpha, beta] when alpha greater than or equal to x. In particular, any interpretation of the underlying decision theory here will have to give some role to 'whim or sentiment or chance', and I give it a variable, 'rho'. With this theory, I have the extensions needed to avoid Runde's objection to Davidson." (Weatherson, 2002, p. 58).

Rho E[0, 1] is nothing more than Keynes' wE[0, 1]. Further, Keynes' w is grounded in a decision theoretic logic, the "conventional coefficient", that is superior to anything presented by Weatherson in his paper. Seventh, Weatherson's entire "analysis" of weight is based on the intellectual quagmire of Runde (1990, 1991), which can be traced back directly to Levi (1967) and Cohen (1986).

10. Conclusion

The errors made about Keynes' concept of weight of evidence have been passed down over a 40 year period in a number of economics and philosophy (and psychology)[2] journals. The term "scientific" requires as a necessary condition error correction. Such an error correction process is not visible in philosophy and economics. They are not scientific.

Of equal concern is the fact that the articles and books exposed in this paper have been cited in the SSCI well over a total of 400 times. This simply means that it is not possible to ever correct these errors. The best approach is to try to quarantine the economics and philosophy professions so as to prevent the spread of further error. Unfortunately, it appears that these errors have now been spread and assimilated in the work of major psychologists. See below.

Footnotes

[1]   See Cole, 2002.

[2]   The psychology literature is becoming as ignorant and error filled as the economics and philosophy literature when it comes to discussing Keynes' contribution to decision theory. It would take a full length paper, greater than the present one, to show this. Therefore, I have selected two sources at random. They are good examples of how the psychology literature evaluates Keynes in a shoddy, shabby, unscientific way.

Consider the errors of Einhorn-Hogarth. They claim "however, it is one thing to acknowledge the importance of ambiguity (of Keynes, 1921, p. 71) and another to develop a theory that incorporates it in the assessment of probabilities and the determination of choices." (p. S229) and

"We are aware of only two other rules for dealing with ambiguous choice, one propounded by Ellsberg . . . and the other by Gardenfors and Sahlin." (p. S244)

The refutation of Einhorn and Hogarth can be found in Sections 7 and 8 of Chapter 26 of the TP. See Section II above.

Now consider the errors of Wallsten:

"The fact that not all uncertainties can be measured by unique probability distributions was noted as early as 1921 by both Knight ([1921] 1971) and Keynes ([1921] 1962). Knight distinguished unmeasurable uncertainty from measurable risk, where the latter includes situations for which probability distributions are available on the basis of a priori calculations or past experience. Keynes argued for three types of uncertainty. In one case, the information base is so weak that an individual cannot determine which of two events is more probable or whether in fact they are equally probable. In a second case, the information base allows a rank ordering of events according to probability but does not support the assignment of numerical values. Finally, "in a very special type of case . . . meaning can be given to a numerical comparison of magnitude" Keynes [1921] 1962, 34). Keynes also suggested that it would occasionally be possible to put bounds on numerical probabilities for events, in which case, he said, the probability is known only vaguely." (Wallsten, 1991, pp. 31-32).

First, there are not three types of uncertainty. Uncertainty (and *not risk*) is measured on the interval [0,1], where w, weight of evidence, [0,1]. Wallsten's discussion is simply confused. All probabilities are of three kinds: rank order, interval (non-numerical) or numerical. Interval estimates are inexact, requiring upper and lower bounds or limits. Numerical probabilities can be precise (law of large numbers and central limit theorem holds) or non precise (use of Chebyshev's Inequality).

Finally, Keynes suggested that it would be possible *in a great many cases* to put bounds on probabilities. *Nowhere* in the TP does Keynes state that such bounded probabilities are "known only vaguely". Thus,

"4. Many probabilities—in fact all those which are equal to the probability of some other argument which has the same premiss and of which the conclusion is incompatible with that of the original argument—

are numerically measurable in the sense that there is *some* other probability with which they are comparable" (Keynes, 1921, p. 159). And

"The sphere of inexact numerical comparison is not, however, quite so limited. Many probabilities, which are incapable of numerical measurement, can be placed nevertheless *between* numerical limits. And by taking particular non-numerical probabilities as standards a great number of comparisons or approximate measurements become possible. If we can place a probability in an order of magnitude with some standard probability, we can obtain its approximate measure by comparison.

This method is frequently adopted in common discourse. When we ask how probable something is, we often put our question in the form—It is more or less probable than so and so ?—where 'so and so' is some comparable and better known probability. We may thus obtain information in cases where it would be impossible to ascribe any *number* to the probability in question." (Keynes, 1921, p. 160).

Vagueness only enters into the discussion when one is attemtping to derive inductive conclusions through analogy (p. 259, TP). Vagueness does not enter into Keynes' discussion on page 34 of the TP, although he does emphasize that probabilities are *between* two numerical measures on pages 32, 34-35 of the TP. Thus, they are non-numerical (i.e., not by a *single* numeral).

References

Ayer, Alfred J. 1972. Probability and Evidence. New York: Columbia University Press.

Cohen L. J. 1986. "Twelve Questions About Keynes's Concept of Weight", Brit. J. Phil. Sci., 37, 263-278.

Cole, K.C. 2002. "What is transparent is our need to see things clearly", LA Times, July 22, 2002, p. A-10.

Cottrell, A. 1993. "Keynes's Theory of Probability and its Relevance to his Economics", Economics and Philosophy, 9, 25-51.

Dow, S. 1995. "Uncertainty about uncertainty". Chapter 7 in Keynes Knowledge and Uncertainty, ed. By S. Dow and J. Hillard. England: Ed. Elgar, pp. 117-127.

Dow, S. 1994. "Uncertainty". In The Elgar Companion to Radical Political Economy. Ed. By P. Arestis and M. Sawyer. Edward Elger, England, pp. 434-438.

Einhorn, H. J. And Hogarth, R.M. (1986). "Decision Making Under Ambiguity", Journal of Business, 59, 5225-5250.

Keynes, J.M. 1921. A Treatise on Probability. London: Macmillan. AMS Edition, 1979. [CWJMK edition, 1973, Vol. 8].

Keynes, J.M. 1964. The General Theory of Employment, Interest, and Money. Harcourt, Brace, and Com.

Lawson, T. 1985. "Uncertainty and economic analysis", Economic Journal, 95, 909-927.

_____1987. "The Relative/Absolute Nature of Knowledge and Economic Analysis", Economic Journal, 97, 951-970.

Levi, I. 1985. "Imprecision and Indeterminacy in Probability Judgment", Philosophy of Science, 52, 390-409.

_____1974. "On Indeterminate Probabilities Journal of Philosophy, 71, 391-418.

_____1967. Gambling With Truth. New York: A. Knopf.

Runde, J. 1990. "Keynesian Uncertainty and the Weight of Arguments", Economics and Philosophy, 6, 275-292.

Runde, J. 1991. "Keynesian Uncertainty and the instability of beliefs", Review of Political Economy, 3, 125-145.

Wallsten, T.S. 1990. "The Costs and Benefits of Vague Information: In Insights in Decision Making", ed. By R.M. Hogarth, Chicago: University of Chicago Press, 28-43.

Weatherson, B. 2002. "Keynes, Uncertainty and Interest Rates", Cambridge Journal of Economics, 26, 47-62.

6

Runde, Mizuhara (2003), the Spread of Error Over Time in Economics and Philosophy Journals and the Failure to Apply Keynes' Decision Theory

Abstract— Eleven of the nineteen essays contained in Runde and Mizuhara are flawed, entirely or in part, by their reliance on an error-filled exposition, originally written by Issac Levi, dealing with J.M. Keynes' 1921 discussion of his "weight of the arguments (weight of the evidence)" in his *Treatise on Probability* (1921). No error correcting mechanism is present in these articles. In fact, just the opposite is occurring. The spread of error over time is multiplying rapidly, similar to the spread of a contagion or epidemic. Such a field can't be deemed scientific or even artistic.

1. Introduction

The Runde-Mizuhara (2003) volume contains three major errors. These errors infect 11 out of the 19 essays. All of the errors can be traced back to Levi in 1967, Lawson in 1985, Runde in 1990, 1991, 1994 a, b and 1995, and Meeks, Carabelli, and O'Donnell in 1976, 1988, and 1989, 1990 respectively.

Section II covers Lawson's error. It is a disguised form of Levi's original error. Section III covers Runde's extensive errors from 1990-1995. Section IV covers the Meeks, Carabelli, and O'Donnell misinterpretation of the diagram on page 39 of the *Treatise on Probability*, 1921 (p. 42 of the 1973 CWJMK edition). A number of other economists have incorrectly used this diagram. However, all such analysis can be traced back to Meeks, Carabelli, and O'Donnell. Section V concludes by considering the role which mathematical, statistical, logical, and probabilistic illiteracy, innumeracy, and ineptness has played over the last seventy years in the sub fields of economic thought, history of economic thought, economic history, economic methodology, and philosophy of economics, as well as in all areas of economic specialization involving J.M. Keynes. These would primarily be the Post Keynesians, Institutionalists, Cambridge Keynesians, and eclectic economists such as Clower, Leijonhufvud, Patinkin, etc.

2. Levi, Lawson, and the Definition of Uncertainty in the TP.

Lawson claimed that "Keynes nowhere explicitly defines uncertainty in A Treatise on Probability" (Lawson, 1985, 913). This is very similar to Levi's claim that Keynes never defined an index to measure weight of evidence in the TP (see essay 18 above). Runde's contributions can thus be seen as a flawed attempt to provide the alleged missing definition of uncertainty by analyzing "weight of evidence" in Chapter 26 of the TP.

Dunn (2003) simply accepts these errors and builds on them (Dunn, 2003, p. 171, 181). Of course, Keynes, on p. 315 (1921; p. 348, 1973) did exactly what it is claimed that he did not do.

> "We could, if we liked, define a conventional coefficient c of weight and risk . . . where w measures the "weight", which is equal to unity when p=1 and w=1, and to zero when p=0 or w=0, *and has an intermediate value in other cases*[2] (author's underscore) (Keynes, 1921, p. 315, 1973, p. 348).

Of course, Keynes *must* do this in order to complete his analysis from the top of p. 315:

> "There seems, at any rate, a good deal to be said for the conclusion that other things being equal, that course of action is preferable which involves least risk (author's note- this type of risk is nonlinear; it is *not* the standard deviation or variance. Keynes analyzes a hybrid of the standard deviation and variance in his R formula on the same page) and about the results of which we have the most complete knowledge. In marginal cases, therefore, the coefficients of weight and risk as well as that of probability are relevant to our conclusions. It seems natural to suppose that they should exert some influence in other case also . . . ." (Keynes, 1921, p. 315).

Keynes' further comments about the problem of measurability cause no problems for a reader of the TP who has grasped Keynes' analysis of interval estimation (approximation) from Chapters 10, 15-17 and 29-30 of the TP. However, it is precisely these chapters that Lawson, Runde, Carabelli, O'Donnell, Meeks, etc., have never covered *or* mentioned in practically all of their work, except as one sentence throw away comments.

Keynes has defined weight of evidence as an index, normalized on the unit interval [0,1]. Thus

$$wE[0,1]$$

or

$$0 \text{ less than or equal to } w \text{ less than or equal to } 1.$$

Consider the following:

> "The results of our endeavors are very uncertain, but we have a genuine probability even when the evidence upon which it is founded is slight. The matter is truly stated by Bishop Butler: 'From our short views it is greatly uncertain . . .

"¹. The difficulties which exist are not chiefly due, I think, to our ignorance of the remote future." (Keynes, 1921, p. 310).

It is obvious that this is where Keynes got the verbiage to use both in Chapters 12-13 of the General Theory (GT) in 1936 and in his 1937 QJE article. Consider the following:

	TP (Ch.26)	GT (1936)	GT (1937)
evidence is:	"very uncertain"	"vague", "scanty",	"vague"
	"slight", "greatly	"very slight",	"uncertain"
	uncertain",	"little"	"flimsy"
	"ignorance"		"we simply
	do not know"		

Keynes (1937), pp. 213-214) provided a descriptive scale measuring the weight of evidence that allows the decision maker to rank uncertainty (weight of evidence). I will show that there is a one-to-one onto correspondence between this scale (discrete) and the continuous index w in the TP that is isomorphic.

First, GT (1937) we have, where U = uncertainty and w = weight of evidence:

U=1.0   U=0

"We simply do not know"	"Moderately Uncertain"	"Slightly Uncertain"	Known For Certain"

Next, the TP (1921):

w=0   W=1.0

"Ignorance"	"Very Uncertain"	"Evidence . . . is slight	"Intermediate value"	"Greater" body of Knowledge"	"High weight
	"Greatly Uncertain"	"The available information is necessarily small"		"Completer Knowledge"	"Most Complete Knowledge"

Letting U=0 ("known for certain") and U=1.0 ("we simply don't know"), we have UE[0,1]. From the TP, we have wE[0,1].

Consider a mapping Q:U as it approaches w. Clearly, the operations of addition and multiplication are preserved under this mapping. Q is a homomorphism. Since Q is also a one-to-one *onto* mapping, that is order and rank preserving, it is also an isomorphism.

What can one make of Lawson's claim? One must assign Lawson's claim a w=0, because "we simply do not know" how Lawson arrived at his claim. Lawson does not have the excuse available to Levi, which was overlooking Chapter 26 of the TP. This observation applies to every philosopher with the exception of William Johnson, whose w=worth of evidence, wE[0,1], is very similar to Keynes' weight of evidence.

Section 3

Runde made a number of unsupported claims in his 1990, 1991 articles. He has incorporated these errors in most of his more recent work. As above, Runde can't claim ignorance of Chapter 26.

> "It is true that he does, in an offhand passage, propose a 'conventional' coefficient of weight and risk. But this is only to set up his conclusion that the DME is unlikely to be saved by attempts to find some more complicated function of the probability where with to compound the proposed good." (Keynes, 1921, pp. 315-316; 1973, p. 348; see Runde 1994b, pp. 114-115).

Again, since w, like p, requires interval estimates and/or upper/lower limits/bounds, Keynes' comment is understandable *if* the reader has already grasped Keynes' theory of approximation. Runde has *not* grasped this point.

Finally, the issue of a conventional coefficient, which, by the way, is superior to any such decision rule derived since the 1979 Kahneman-Tversky article in *Econometrica*, is separate from the issue of defining a weight of index. Runde reads, but does not understand. Runde need only have reported back to Lawson that Keynes had already correctly defined w on p. 315 of the 1921 edition of the TP (1973, p. 348).

In Runde, 1990, pp. 280-283, it is claimed that Keynes had three different definitions of weight. Three different definitions would mean that Keynes was inconsistent. In fact, Keynes demonstrates that the one (consistent) definition he gave, $0 \leq w \leq 1$, has three different *applications*. Only in the minds of Lawson, Runde, and the economists they have confused are there three different definitions. Runde should have been able to catch his errors, which are grade school level. He puts forth three different "equations". First, he proposes that V(X/h) (Keynes' V(a/h)) is

$$V(X/h) = K_r/I_r.$$

This makes no sense. Further, it can't be normalized, since if there is complete knowledge, $I_r=0$ and $K_r=1$. However, 1/0 is undefined.

Second, he proposes

$$V(X/h) = K_r/(K_r+I_r)$$
$$= 1/(w+1)$$
where $w=I_r/K_r$.

Again, the problem arises if there is complete ignorance. As above, $I_r=1$ and $K_r=0$. But 1/0 is undefined.

Finally, Runde settles on

$$V(X/h) = K_r/(K_r+I_r).$$

This doesn't work either. Keynes denotes $h_1(h_2)$ to represent single unit of information or individual fact. h represents a fixed amount of evidence. Thus, Runde needs to write in his notation

$$V(X/hh_1h_2 \ldots h_nh_{n+1}) = K_r/(K_r+I_r).$$

Also, Runde needs to state that he is normalizing V on the unit interval, so that

0 less than or equal to V less than or equal to 1.

But then it is easy to see that this is identical to Keynes' result in Chapter 26, which was

0 less than or equal to w less than or equal to 1.

Thus, Runde and Mizuhara 2003, p. 4; Meeks 2003, p. 28, p. 30; McCann, Jr., pp. 44-45; Runde 2003, p. 48, p. 52; Davis 2003, p. 100, p. 102; Gillies 2003, p. 113; Fioretti 2003, p. 134; Winslow 2003, p. 147, p. 156; Dunn 2003, p. 171, p. 181; Mizuhara 2003, p. 200, pp. 202-203; Dow 2003, p. 209; and Gerrard 2003, pp. 240-241 all pass on the original errors in Runde, 1990.

Gerrard (2003) states,

> "Despite the practical importance that Keynes attached to the concept, he did not define the weight of argument consistently throughout the *Treatise*. As Runde (1990) has argued, Keynes variously defined the weight of argument as (1) the absolute amount of relevant evidence, (2) the degree of completeness of the evidence, and (3) the balance of absolute amounts of relevant knowledge and relevant ignorance, on which a probability is based. The latter two definitions measure evidence relative to ignorance. The differences between the three definitions are not merely a matter of semantics. They differ in their operational implications. Whereas an increase in the amount of relevant evidence necessarily increases weight under definition (1), it does not necessarily imply so under definitions (2) and (3). Indeed, if additional relevant evidence indicates that there is considerably more ignorance than previously believed, then under definitions (2) and (3) the weight of argument may be reduced." (Gerrard, 2003, p. 241).

On the next page, we find Gerrard writing the following:

> "According to Keynes, then, the doctrine of mathematical expectation is inadequate as an explanation of

human behavior under conditions of uncertainty. He argued for the need to develop a more general theory of behavior under uncertainty. Such a theory would involve at least four determinants of the choice between alternative courses of action: (1) degree of goodness, (2) probability, (3) weight, and (4) risk. Keynes explored the possibility of using a more complicated function of probability that incorporated weight and risk effects, suggesting a 'conventional coefficient' c defined as:

$$c=2pw(1+q)(1+w)$$

where p is the probability, w is the weight of the available evidence and q (=1-p) is the risk. The conventional coefficient ranges from unity when there is full information (w=1) and full belief (p=1) to zero when there is no evidence (w=0) and no degree of belief (p=0). Keynes considered using the conventional expectation, cA, as the general theory of behavior under uncertainty. However, he concluded that it is unlikely to be useful to formulate the conventional coefficient in a precise mathematical form, given the implied uniformity of behavior and the problems of measuring goodness, probability and weight." (Gerrard, 2003, p. 242).

There are a number of errors, as well as a logical conflict between the two pages of Gerrard's article. First, the goal is to maximize cA, where A stands for outcome. If one is dealing with ethics or moral philosophy, then A is the *amount* of goodness, not the degree of goodness. Second, c is mis-specified.

$$c=2pw/(1+q)(1+w)$$
and not $c=2pw(1+q)(1+w)$.

Third, q(=1-p) is *not* the risk in the c coefficient formula. In Keynes' R=qpA formula, qEMV measures the risk. In the c coefficient, risk, representing nonlinear probability preferences, is given by the weight $(1/(1+q))\cdot EMV(=pA)$ or as

$$cA=pA/(1+q)$$

where, w.l.o.g., we set w=1.0. This would hold for a risk averse decision maker. For a risk taker

$$cA=pA(1+q).$$

For a risk neutral state,

$$cA=pA.$$

Fourth, c does not equal 0 when "(w=0) and . . . (p=0)" (Gerrard, 2003, p. 242). c=0 when w=0 *or* p=0. If w=0, then no p can be calculated, since there is *no* evidence.

Finally, Gerrard errs in leaving out the fact that c ". . . has an intermediate value in other cases" (Keynes, 1921, p. 315), i.e., for w *between* 0 and 1 and p between 0 and 1. We now deal with Gerrard's logical contradiction. If Keynes has defined w such that w can equal 1, 0 or have intermediate values, between 0 and 1, then Keynes has provided an index for weight of evidence and Runde's musings are just errors. If Runde is correct, then it makes no sense for Gerrard to discuss Keynes' c coefficient, because supposedly, Keynes did not define a index for evidential weight, i.e., w.

4. Keynes "Non-Numerical" Probability and the Diagram on p. 39 (1921) or p. 42 (1973) of the *TP*.

According to Meeks (2003, p. 35), O'Donnell (1989, p. 55), O'Donnell (1990, p. 33), and Carabelli (1988, p. 49), the diagram on p. 39 (1921) or p. 42 (1973) "explains" Keynes' views on "non-numerical" probabilities, orderings, un-or noncomparability and

un-or nonmeasurability. Contrary to these authors, this chapter is
an introductory chapter. It is not "the chapter on the measurement
of probability", (Carabelli, p. 48). Nowhere in the rest of the TP
does Keynes refer back to this diagram. Nowhere do Meeks,
O'Donnell, or Carabelli mention or deal with Keynes' theory of
approximation (intervals, upper/lower limits/bounds). O'Donnell
limits his discussion of Chapters 15 and 17 of the TP to the following
footnote (O'Donnell, 1990, p. 37)

> "For further remarks on numerical probabilities, see TP
> ch. 15 . . . for an account of Keynes' principles of comparison
> for numerical and non-numerical probabilities, see
> O'Donnell (1982 ?) Ch. 3."

However, when one turns to Chapter 3, one finds a one-half
page throw-away discussion titled "Inexact or Approximate
Comparison" (O'Donnell, 1989, p. 60). Nowhere is there any
discussion of the theory of approximation or of finite probabilities.
Nowhere is there any modification of the conclusions reached by
O'Donnell based on the diagram on p. 39 (1921, TP). There is no
mention of George Boole anywhere in either O'Donnell's book or
article. Meeks and Carabelli are similarly deficient.

Contrary to Fioretti, Keynes developed the idea of non-
numerical probability *measurement* from Boole. Boole allowed for
indeterminate probabilities. Thus "Minor" and "Superior" limiting
values could be derived (Boole, 1854, p. 268, 277).

Keynes points out that in using Boole's techniques

> ". . . we are apt to be left with an equation of the second
> or of an even higher degree . . ." (Keynes, 1921, p. 161).

The four curvatures in Keynes' diagram are all either quadratic
or can be approximated by quadratic equations. The point A
intersects (0,1) at roughly .65. One can solve the quadratic
equations. For OVA, A is an upper bound. Solving the quadratic

equations for the vertex allows one to narrow the upper and/or lower bounds by using the line of symmetry plus the roots 0 and 1 (or 0 and .65). Keynes' conclusion that

> "Many probabilities, which are incapable of numerical measurement, can be placed nevertheless *between* (Keynes' emphasis) numerical limits." (Keynes, 1921, p. 160)

represents a total, complete and final refutation of the mathematically inept claims of Meeks, Carabelli, and O'Donnell, some 60 years before their books/articles were published.

What would Keynes say today? Well, he would say that most probabilities *are* "non-numerical", but that most probabilities have upper/lower limits, excluding the trivial cases of a lower limit of 0 and a upper limit of 1 or a lower limit >0 and an upper limit <1. He might also suggest to just take the mid-point, or better yet, use Chebyshev's inequality.

Keynes would also acknowledge the work of several researchers who have successfully built on Keynes' foundation of partial orders, interval estimates, non additive, non-linear decision weights and indices for weight of evidence, o less than or equal to w less than or equal to 1, where

$$w = k_1/k_1 + I_1$$

and changes in w are a function of change in the amount of single units of positive and negative data through his V relation of weight of the argument, i.e., $V(a/hh_1h_2h_3 \ldots h_{n+1}) > V(ah)$, where h_1, h_{n+1}, are relevant amounts of evidence and the $h_i, i = 1, n+1$, are single units of information, either positive or negative.

In the area of interval estimtes, Halparin and Walley would be acknowledged. In the area of indexing the weight of evidence, Wang (2001) would receive a "thumbs up". Wang also deserves credit for pointing out the flaw in Dempster-Shafer belief functions.[1] The reader should note, however, that neither Walley nor Wang are aware of how advanced, detailed, and modern Keynes' 1921 approach is, especially when updated to include the heuristics and conventions described by Keynes in great detail in Chapter 12 of the GT. For instance, Walley states,

> "The following introduction outlines the main concepts
> of the theory of Walley (1991) . . . which is based on earlier
> ideas of Keynes (1921) . . . Smith (1961) . . ." (Walley, 1998,
> p. 1).

Keynes is not mentioned again in the paper.

Wang (2001) gives a quote from Chapter 6, p. 71 of the TP, but does not include any chapter or page reference to the quote. Nor does he discuss Keynes' V relation of Chapter 6 or Keynes' index for weight of evidence (in Chapter 26), w, or Keynes' decision rule c. This leads me to conclude that much of what Walley and Wang think is original in their work is already available in Keynes' work.

It should also be mentioned that Peirce's measure for weight of evidence or reliability of evidence, the standard error of the estimate, $sigma/(n)^{1/2}$, is "a good practical measure of the weight", "due to the fact that in scientific problems at large probable (standard) error is . . . due to a great lack of evidence, and that as the available evidence increases there is a tendency for the probable error to diminish" (Keynes, 1921, p. 75). However, Wang's reference to Peirce is incorrect if what Wang is asserting is that Peirce constructed an *index* to measure weight of evidence *separate* from any probability concept. Sigma is a probability concept and hence is, strictly speaking, not a completely separate second number or concept.

Finally, Wang overlooks William Johnson's 1932 specification of a variable to measure the *worth* of the evidence. Johnson calls this w, where $0<w<1$. Wang should also note that Carnap's continuum of inductive logics harks back to a very similar construction made by Johnson in his 1932 Philosophy of Science article.

5. The Future of Heterodox Schools of Economics

This author sees a very grim future for the heterodox schools of economics. This is due to a very simple observable fact. 99% of the members of these schools suffer from one of the following afflictions:

A. Mathematical Illiteracy
B. Statistical Illiteracy
C. Logical Illiteracy
D. Probabilistic Illiteracy

A good 80% suffer all four afflictions simultaneously. They spend their time lecturing their fellow illiterates that JM Keynes was anti-mathematical or that he was against formalism, or Keynes was opposed to statistical and/or econometric analysis. Of course, we discover that Keynes "was a poor mathematician by 1927" and that he didn't know how to present the theory of effective demand correctly because he forgot to correctly specify the aggregate supply function Z=h(N) in Chapter 3 of the GT. All of the above is simple intellectual garbage, manufactured by one of the most mathematically illiterate of economists, Joan Robinson.

This does not mean that heterodox economics will become extinct. They will always be able to attract enough mathematically illiterate followers to pass the baton on to the next generation. But as far as having any real, even if minor, influence on the real world, the probability is 0, while w=1.

6. Conclusions

It is now time to list the innovations made by J.M. Keynes in applied probability theory, decision theory, and applied statistics.

(a) Applied Probability Theory

J. M. Keynes was the first theorist to state that the probability relation is one of *partial* entailment or order. This automatically led to Keynes' adaptation of Boole's technique, and others of his own invention, in order to specify the concept of *interval* estimates. Obviously, if there is *any* overlap whatsoever, then the probabilities are *non-comparable* and *non-rankable* by "<", ">", "less than or equal to", "greater than or equal to".

Similarly, intervals are *non-additive* and/or *sub* or super *additive*, although Keynes made headway in Chapter 12 of the TP on pages 133, 136-138, on this topic. Keynes also incorporates *irrational* numbers into the body of probabilities since they can be bounded from above/below.

Unfortunately, Keynes called his interval estimates "non-numerical probabilities". This term has been completely misinterpreted by every economist who has written on the TP, as well as many philosophers who should have known better. "Non-numerical" means "*not by a single number*", but by "*two numbers*".

Finally, it was Keynes who put forth the first conceptualization of *conflicting evidence* (Keynes, 1921, p. 30) with his dark clouds-raining-barometer problem. Here, since there is *no* overlap in the evidence, the two probabilities are non-comparable. This problem is very similar to the blue-red Morocco-calf book problem in the same chapter.

(b) Decision Theory

Keynes' specification of an index to measure weight of evidence and his incorporation of such an index into his conventional coefficient of risk and weight solves the following "paradoxes" and "anomolies" of "modern" decision theory:

— The Ellsberg Paradox
— The Fellner Paradox
— The Popper Paradox
— The Kunreuther Paradox and assorted "insurance" paradoxes.
— The certainty effect
— The reflection effect
— The translation effect
— The "common consequences" or "common ratios" effect.
— The fanning out effect

— The preference reversal anomaly
— Many of the so-called behavioral finance anomalies, such as the equity risk premium paradox, once Keynes' discussions of conventions in Chapter 12 of the GT is added to his approach to probability and decision.
— Keynes' approach solves the problem of the blue-green taxis put forth by Tversky and Kahneman in 1973-75, which set off a 20 year series of exchanges with L.J. Cohen, primarily in *Brain and Behavioral Science*. Tversky capitulated to Cohen in 1994 by explicitly proclaiming to have established support theory. The degree of support, of course, was defined to be between 0 and 1, 0 signifying no evidentiary support and 1 signifying that a proposition had full evidentiary support. Of course, Tversky's degree of support is identical to Keynes degree of weight of evidence, w, defined to be between 0 and 1.

(c) Applied Statistics

— Keynes' advocacy of Cheybshev's inequality as a way of dealing with skewness and kurtosis in decision making is superior to the current endemic use of the normal probability distribution. Unless the law of large numbers and CLT hold in the strong sense, Cheybshev's inequality can give a *lower* bound while the N.D. gives an upper bound.
— Keynes' advocacy of the Lexis Q Test in order to test for the dynamic stability of an econometric multiple regression equation put him far ahead of Tinbergen and Frisch, 1939-40.

References

Brady, Michael E. (1993). "J.M. Keynes' Theoretical Approach to Decision-Making Under Conditions of Risk and Uncertainty", Brit. J. Phil. Sci., 44, 357-376.

Brady, Michael E. (2002). "Further Applications of J.M. Keynes' Approach to Decision-Making Under Risk and Uncertainty", Inter. J. Of App. Econ. And Econometrics, 10, 431-462.

Brady, Michael E. (2003). "How Issac Levi Gambled With The Truth and Lost Badly: Why Philosophy and Economics Fail to Satisfy the Necessary 'Transparency' Condition to be Considered Scientific", In Brady, 2003. Pennsylvania: Xlibris Press.

Carabelli, A. (1988). "On Keynes' Method", London: Macmillan.

Davis, J.B. (2003). "The Relationship Between Keynes' Early and Later Philosophical Thinking", In Runde and Mizuhara, 2003, 100-110.

Dow, S.C. (2003). "Probability, Uncertainty and Convention . . .", In Runde and Mizuhara, 2003, 207-215.

Dunn, S.P. (2003). "Keynes and Transformation", In Runde and Mizuhara, 2003, 170-181.

Fioretti, G. (2003). "No Faith, No Conversion . . .", In Runde and Mizuhara, 2003, 130-139.

Fioretti, G. (2001). "Von Kries and the Other 'German Logicians': Non-Numerical Probabilities Before Keynes", Economics and Philosophy, 17, 245,273.

Fioretti, G. (1998). "John Maynard Keynes and Johannes Von Kries", History of Economic Ideas, 6, 51-80.

Gerrard, Bill (2003). "Keynesian Uncertainty: What Do We Know?", In Runde and Mizuhara, 2003, 239-251.

Hailperin, T. (1976). Boole's Logic and Probability. Studies in logic and the foundations of Mathematics; Vol. 85. North Holland: Amsterdam.

Hansen, P. and B. Jaumard. (1997). "Probabilistic Satisfiability". Unpublished paper.

Keynes, J.M. (1937). "The General Theory of Employment", QJE, 51, 209-223.

Keynes, J.M. (1936). "The General Theory of Employment, Interest, and Money", Harcourt, Brace and Company.

Keynes, J.M. (1921). "A Treatise on Probability", London: MacMillan.

Levi, Issac (1967). Gambling With Truth, NY: A. Knopf.

Levi, Issac (1974). "Indeterminate Probabilities", The Journal of Philosophy, 71, 391-418.

Lawson, T. (1985). "Uncertainty and Economic Analysis", Economic Journal, 95, 909-927.

McCann, Jr., C.R. (2003). "On the Nature of Keynesian Probability", In Runde and Mizuhara, 2003, 37-45.

Meeks, G.T. (2003). "Keynes on the Rationality of Decision Procedures Under Uncertainty: The Investment Decision", In Runde and Mizuhara, 2003, 19-36.

Mizuhara, S. (2003). "Keynesian Convention: A Textual Note", In Runde and Mizuhara, 2003, 196-204.

O'Donnell, R.M. (1989). "Keynes: Philosophy Economics and Politics", London: MacMillan.

_____(1990). "Keynes on Mathematics: Philosophical Foundations and Economic Applications", Cambridge Journal of Economics, 14, 29-47.

Runde, J and Mizuhara, S., ed. (2003). "The Philosophy of Keynes' Economics: Probability, Uncertainty, and Convention", New York: Routledge.

_____"Introduction", In Runde and Mizuhara, 2003, 1-16.

Runde, J. (2003). "On Some Explicit Links Between Keynes' *A Treatise on Probability* and *The General Theory*, in Runde and Mizuhara, 2003, 46-54.

_____(1991). "Keynesian Uncertainty and the Instability of Beliefs", Review of Political Economy, 3, 125-145.

_____(1994a). "Keynesian Uncertainty and Liquidity Preference", Cambridge Journal of Economics, 18, 129-144.

_____(1994b). "Keynes After Ramsey: In Defense of *A Treatise on Probability*", Studies in History and Philosophy of Science, 25, 97-121.

_____(1995). "Risk, Uncertainty and Bayesian Decision Theory: A Keynesian View", In Dow and Hillard (eds.), 1995.

Shafer, G. (1976). A Mathematical Theory of Evidence. New Jersey: Princeton Univ. Press.

Wang, P. (2001). "Confidence as Higher-Order Uncertainty".
Presented at 2nd International Symposium on Imprecise
probabilities and Their Applications, Ithaca, NY. Also
published as Wang, P. (1994a), Confidence as higher order
uncertainty. Technical Report 93, Center for Research on
Concepts and Cognition, Indiana University, Bloomington,
Indiana.

Wang, P. (1994). "A Defect in Dempster-Shafer Theory". In
Proceedings of the Tenth Conference on Uncertainty in
Artificial Intelligence, pp. 560-66. M. Kaufmann: California.

Winslow, T. (2003). "The Foundations of Keynes' Economics", In
Runde and Mizuhara.

Footnote

[1]   There are a number of historically inaccurate assessments and conclusions
made by G. Shafer (1976) implicitly about J.M. Keynes and explicitly
about L.J. Cohen:

> "In fact, almost all Twentieth Century Bayesians have
> explicitly advocated one or the other of the two alternatives
> I have just rejected. Either they have followed Harold Jeffreys
> and John Maynard Keynes in insisting that numerical
> degrees of support are indeed objectively determined by
> given evidence, or else they have followed . . . Ramsey . . .
> and deFinetti . . . ." (Shafer, 1976, p. 21).

Shafer is simply wrong. Keynes insisted that there were numerical OR
NON NUMERICAL degrees of support. Nor does Shafer have any idea of
the role played by Boole in Keynes' approach, i.e., interval estimates.
Nowhere in Shafer's book does he ever mention or discuss Keynes' Theory
of Evidential Weight. If he had done so, he would have realized that an
application of Occam's Razor would reveal Keynes' theory to be superior to
his own. This brings us to Shafer's discussion of L.J. Cohen and GLS
Shackle. It was widely known at the time Shafer was writing his book that

Cohen, following Keynes' conception, would have a completely different interpretation from Shackle (see Cohen, 1980, p. 171) or Levi-Shackle, i.e., Cohen's Baconian functions are about reality while Levi-Shackle functions are about "our thoughts about" reality, i.e., Shafer's belief function(s) specified under a particular set of beliefs. On page 225, Shafer essentially admits that his theory and Shackle's are very close for the case of non-conflicting evidence assessments:

> Mr. Shackle . . . relies instead (of evidence) on direct speculation about how partial beliefs ought to behave. He usually writes about the "degree of potential surprise" associated with a proposition, a quantity that corresponds to the degree of doubt Dou (A) = BeL(Ä) of our theory, both in its intuitive meaning and its relation to the degree of belief. And he explicitly imposes on these degrees of potential surprise the two rules listed in Theorem 10.5.

Given the closeness of Shafer and Shackle, it should not surprise the reader that Shafer states, in relation to Cohen's views, that,

> I may be quite off the mark in my interpretation of Cohen's ideas, for I often find his meaning obscure" (Shafer, 1976, p. 225).

Shafer is off the mark. Keynes includes both dissonance and consonance in his threory of probability, as well as in his theory of evidential weight *when specified mathematically as an index of weight of evidence* in Chapter 26 of the TP. In fact, Keynes is the first scholar to not just mention conflicting evidence, but to *emphasize* it.

7

A Note on Keynes' Page 39 (Page 42)

Diagram in the 1921 (1973) Edition of the

A Treatise on Probability (TP): Correcting the

Logical Errors of G. Meeks, A. Carabelli,

and R. O'Donnell

Abstract— Keynes, in his introductory Chapter 3 of the TP, provided an introductory graphical illustration of his upper lower bound interval approach which he called approximation. Approximation is the foundation of Keynes' finite probabilities approach to induction and analogy. Keynes' approximation approach is based on Boolean probability logic. This approach, covered by Keynes in Chapters 15-17 of the TP, requires the solution of 2nd order (and some nth order) quadratic equations. The shape will be non linear (parabolic), reflecting non-linear probability preferences. Meeks, Carabelli and O'Donnell either ignore or are ignorant of Keynes' approach. They base their claims on the above mentioned diagram. Boole does not appear in any of their bibliographies. Nor does Chapters 15-17 of the TP appear except in a one-half page throw away comment by O'Donnell (1989).

1. Introduction

This paper is organized in the following fashion. We will cover Keynes' interval approach in Chapter 3, tie it to his discussion of non-linear probability preferences in Chapter 26 and again note that Keynes has a theory of approximation developed in Chapters 15-17 of the TP, that allows one to calculate upper-lower limits, i.e., intervals. We will then cover the errors of Meeks, Carabelli, and O'Donnell. We sum up in a concluding section.

2. Discussion of intervals in Chapter III of the TP.

2a) Intervals.

"Underwriters are actually willing . . . to name a numerical measure in every case and to back their opinion with money. But this practice shows no more than that many probabilities are greater or less than some numerical measure, not that they are numerically definite" (Keynes, 1921, p. 22).

"In fact, underwriters themselves distinguish between risks which are properly insurable, either because their probability can be estimated between comparatively narrow numerical limits . . . and other risks which can not be dealt with in this way . . ." (Keynes, 1921, p. 23).

"A distinction, interesting for our present purpose, between probabilities, which can be estimated within somewhat narrow limits, and those which cannot, ..." (Keynes, 1921, p. 24).

"A relation of probability does not yield us, as a rule, information of much value, unless it invests the conclusion with a probability which lies between narrow numerical limits" (Keynes, 1921, p. 31).

"We frame two ideal arguments . . . in which . . . the evidence largely resembles what is actually within our knowledge, but which is so constituted as to yield a numerical value, and we judge that the probability of the actual argument lies between these two. Since our standards, therefore, are referred to numerical measures in many cases where actual measurement is impossible, and since the probability lies *between* two numerical measures . . ." (Keynes, 1921, p. 32).

Thus, just from Chapter 3 alone, a reader should be able to come to the conclusion that, for Keynes, there are two types of probabilities, definite, exact, precise numerical probabilities and indefinite, inexact, indeterminate non-numerical probabilities, i.e., intervals.

2b) Intervals Estimates May Overlap.

Obviously, intervals are non-additive. If the intervals overlap, "no comparison of magnitude is possible" (Keynes, 1921, p. 34) and "not all probabilities are comparable in respect of more or less"; "it is not always possible to say that the degree of our rational belief is one conclusion is either equal to, greater than, or less than the degree of our belief in another" (Keynes, 1921, p. 34).

In conclusion, interval estimates, *if they overlap*, are non-additive, non-comparable and non-measurable in the usual sense. Intervals are "numerically indeterminate" (Keynes, 1921, p. 34).

2c). Interval Estimates May be Piece-wise Linear or Non-Linear.

In his diagram on 39 (TP, 1921), Keynes has four different non-linear parabolas (second order quadratic equations) representing his non-numerical probabilities. The solutions can be either rational or irrational numbers. Keynes, unfortunately, did not include an example of a piece-wise linear interval. The shapes also demonstrate non-linear probability preferences-the decision maker prefers high probabilities to low probabilities, irrespective of the relative size of the possible outcomes. The continuous linear line OAI, represents unique, linear, additive, exact, single, rational number probabilities.

Keynes extends his discussion of the issues raised in Chapter III in Chapter 26, sections 6-8. Thus,

> ". . . even if a meaning can be given to the sum of a series of non-numerical 'mathematical expectations' not every pair of such sums are numerically comparable in respect of more and less" (Keynes, 1921, p. 312).

and,

> "The last difficulty concerns the question whether . . . the 'mathematical expectation' . . . accurately measures what our preferences ought to be-whether . . . the undesirability of a given course of action increases in direct proportion to any increase in the uncertainty of its attaining its object, or . . . its undesirability increasing more than in proportion to its uncertainty" (Keynes, p. 313, 1921).

Keynes incorporates this type of non linearity in his coefficient, c, by multiplying p by $(1/(1+q))$. If the increase is less than proportional, p is multiplied by $(1+q)$.

2d) Approximation.

In Chapters 15-17, Keynes discusses Boole's technique and adapts it to the determination of interval estimates. The technique requires familiarity with Boolean algebra and is difficult. The modern approach solves these problems by the use of linear programming, simplex method and integer programming. Hailperin made the break through in 1965.

3. The Errors of Meeks

Meeks builds the foundation of her paper (2003; see also 1991) on the last five pages of Chapter III of the TP. After giving Keynes' barometer-black clouds example of conflicting evidence, she concludes,

"There is much more to Keynes' analysis of probability
(for the full story see CWVIII, especially Part I, Chapter
3).[15]" (Meeks, 2003, p. 30).

Nowhere in Meeks article is the reader given any discussion about Keynes' interval estimate approach. In fact, none of Keynes' Chapter III quotations on intervals is ever mentioned. Keynes' discussion in Chapters 5, 10, 15, 16, 17, 20, 21, 22, and 26 of the TP on approximation, finite probabilities, inexact measurement, non linear probability preferences, the "c" coefficient and the relation of Part III of the TP's analysis of analogy and induction to approximation and finite probabilities, is completely overlooked by Meeks. In fact, in Runde and Mizuhara, Boole's name is not mentioned a single time.

Meeks' paper should never have been published either in 1991 or 2003. The claim that "the full story" is contained in "Part I, Chapter 3" is as nonsensical as the claims of Dennis Robertson, Harry Johnson, and Paul Davidson that pages 24-30 of Chapter III of the General Theory contains Keynes' theory of effective demand.

4. The Errors of Carabelli

Carabelli, like Meeks before her, commits the same logical error. First, she does give one of the quotes listed above in Chapter III of the TP, dealing with numerical limits (Carabelli, 1988, p. 47), but its logic completely eludes her. There is not a single reference to interval estimates and/or Boole in her entire book. Carabelli thus interprets "non-numerical measurability and non-comparability of probability" (Carabelli, p. 42) to mean that *no numbers at all*, not one number, not two numbers, not limits or bounds are used by Keynes.

"Keynes' thesis of the ultimate unmeasurability and
incomparability of probability had notable consequences
for the rest of his doctrine" (Carabelli, p. 49).

This "conclusion" follows from her Meeksian "analysis of the diagram" on page 39 (pg. 42, 1973) of the 1921 edition of the TP.

Carabelli has no idea of what she is talking about. She fails to mention that pt.A in the diagram is an obvious upper bound on the "non-numerical probability" V. Pt.A is also a lower bound for "non-numerical" probabilities W, X and Y, given that W is the vertex of an approximate quadratic equation and is the maximum point. Similar errors appear in Chapter 8 of Carabelli's book. Again, as with Meeks, these chapters should not have been published in their present form. The conclusions reached with respect to Meeks apply equally to Carabelli.

5. The Errors of O'Donnell

Nowhere in O'Donnell, 1990, is he aware that Keynes' diagram, which O'Donnell reproduces on page 33 of his article, is meant to represent non linear probability preferences and the use of interval estimates. His footnote 1 states,

> "For further remarks on numerical probabilities, see TP
> Ch. 15" (O'Donnell, 1990, p. 33).

Of course, Chapter 15 deals with the theory of approximation for "non-numerical" probabilities, as does parts of Chapter 16 and 17.

Continuing, O'Donnell writes,

> "For an account of Keynes' principles of comparison
> for numerical and non-numerical probabilities, see
> O'Donnell (1982) ch. 3" (O'Donnell, 1990, p. 33).

However, this discussion is identical to the one page account in Chapter 3 of O'Donnell, 1989, p. 60, titled "Inexact or Approximate Comparison". However, O'Donnell's brief discussion directly conflicts with his earlier statements on pages 52-55, 58-59, as well as omitting any reference to Boole's method, which is what Keynes means by approximation.

Nor is it true that the theory of approximation requires "the non-numerical probability paths will have to cut the numerical path OAI at least once . . ." (O'Donnell, 1989, p. 60). All of Keynes' "non-numerical probabilities" lie on approximate parabolas given by approximate quadratic, second order equations. The roots, be they rational or irrational, can be used to specify upper and/or lower bounds.

6. Conclusions

During the last 25 years, a number of strange articles and books have appeared in the field of economics which make little or no sense. Starting with the strange claims made by Stohs and Garner in 1981 and 1983 in the journal *History of Political Economy* concerning "what is a non-numerical probability?" through Lawson, Runde, O'Donnell, Meeks, Carabelli to Fioretti and Weatherson in the *Cambridge Journal of Economics* in 2002 with his claim about non-numerical probabilities that "are left largely unexplained" (Weatherson 2002, p. 53) or "his mysterious non-numerical values" (Weatherson, p. 53) we end with Weatherson's comic, but tragic, conclusion that Keynes' non-numerical probabilities can be modeled as intervals, based on the work of P. Walley, who has based his work on Boole!!!!

Weatherson is correct. Keynesian probabilities, for the most part, *are interval estimates*. However, it shouldn't take 82 years for the economics and philosophy professions to come to a conclusion that is explicit in the *TP* in 1921.

References

Boole, G. (1854). The Laws of Thought. New York: Dover Publications edition, 1958.

Carabelli, A. (1988). On Keynes' Method. London: Macmillan.

Garner, C. (1983). "Uncertainty in Keynes' General Theory: A Comment", History of Political Economy, 15, 83-86.

Keynes, J.M. (1921). A Treatise on Probability. London: Macmillan (AMS reprinted, 1979).

Keynes, J.M. (1973). A Treatise on Probability. London: Macmillan. Volume 8. CWJMK.

Meeks, J. G.T. (1991). "Keynes on the Rationality of Decision Procedures Under Uncertainty: The Investment Decision". In JGT Meeks (ed.) 1991.

Meeks, J. G.T. (1991). Thoughtful Economic Man: Essays on Rationality, Moral Rules and Benevolence. Cambridge: Cambridge University Press.

Meeks, G.T. (2003). "Keynes on the Rationality of Decision Procedures Under Uncertainty: The Investment Decision". In JGT Meeks (ed.) 1991, pp. 19-36. In the philosophy of Keynes' economics: probability, uncertainty, and convention. Ed. By J. Runde and S. Mizuhara. Routledge: London.

O'Donnell, R.M. (1989). Keynes: Philosophy, Economics and Politics. London: Macmillan.

O'Donnell, R.M. (1990). "Keynes on Mathematics: Philosophical Foundations and Economic Applications", WJE, 14, 29-47.

Stohs, M. (1980). "Uncertainty in Keynes' General Theory", History of Political Economy, 12, 372-382.

Stohs, M. (1983). "Uncertainty in Keynes' General Theory: A Rejoinder", History of Political Economy, 15, 87-91.

Weatherson, B. (2002). "Keynes, Uncertainty, and Interest Rates", Cambridge Journal of Economics, 26, 47-62.

8

The Future of Keynes' Logical Theory of Probability, "Non-Numerical" Probabilities and Conventional Coefficient of Risk and Weight is in AI, Fuzzy Logic, Possibility Theory and Boolean Probability Logic, not in Economics in general and Post Keynesian Economics in Particular

Abstract— Implicitly or explicitly, the fields of artificial intelligence, possibility theory, fuzzy logic and Boolean probability logic make heavy use of the analytic concepts and framework developed by J.M. Keynes in his Treatise on Probability (1921), whether they wish to acknowledge the fact or not. The Post Keynesian, institutionalist and Cambridge neo Keynesian approaches are hopelessly flawed and riddled with error. This is due to their attempt to read difficult mathematical analysis while simultaneously being mathematically illiterate, innumerate and inept. The result is another "what did Keynes really mean?" fiasco, similar to the aggregate supply function-curve fiasco created by D. Robertson, H. Johnson, R. Hawtrey, Joan Robinson, R. Kahn, and P. Davidson.

1. Introduction

I n our last essay, we stopped at a point in time—1921— where, in order to obtain bounds for Keynes' "non-numerical" probabilities, one had to make use of Boole's (Keynes') very difficult technique of eliminating variables if the problem was linear (1st order) and dealt only with marginal probabilities or solving for the roots of 2nd order (quadratic) to nth order equations if the problems also dealt with conditional probabilities.[1] It was suggested that solving for the vertex and line of symmetry also should lead to the specification of upper-lower limits or bounds (intervals).

Fortunately, much progress has been made in terms of devising solution techniques which are much less difficult to use than those used by Keynes and derived from Boole in Chapters XV, XVI, and XVIII of the TP.

Hailperin's Boolean probability approach (1965, 1976) showed how Boole's problems (and hence Keynes' also) could be translated into a basic type of linear programming problem. Both fuzzy logic and possibility theory also essentially make use of linear programming techniques (see Zadeh, 1978 and Zimmermann, 1985). Basic linear, quadratic, integer, recursive, iterative, and hyperbolic programming techniques, combined with advanced simplex solution techniques, have made Keynes' logical probability approach a reality over the last 30 years.

Hanson and Jaumard (1996, p. 12-13, 18) give the updated version of Boole's challenge problem, which is correctly solved by Keynes on pages 187-188 of the TP (1921).[2] Hanson and Jaumard demonstrate Hailperin's techniques of transforming Boolean (Keynesian) probability problems into linear programming problems (Hanson and Jaumard, 1996, p. 13). Hanson and Jaumard also show how to integrate Keynes' weight of the evidence variable, w, or Johnson's worth of the evidence variable, w, into the linear programming set up: In Section 5 of their paper, titled "Nonmonotonic Reasoning and Restoring Satisfiability",

Subsection 5.1, titled "Minimal Extension of Probability Intervals", Hansen and Jaumard show that,

> "When new sentences and their probabilities are added to a probabilistic satisfiability problem, consistency of the resulting system must be checked . . . it suffices, while adding one sentence at a time, to choose a probability pi_{m+1} within the interval [lower pi_{m+1}, upper pi_{m+1}]. However, this might not correspond to the subjective view about pi_{m+1} to be modelled, the sign that some previously chosen values should be revised. This situation is more likely to happen if several new sentences are simultaneously added, possibly by different experts.
>
> Two natural ways to restore satisfiability are to modify the probabilities "$_i$, (or their bounds "$_i$ and "$_i$) and to delete some of the sentences . . . To restore satisfiability (or coherence) with minimal changes one must solve the following linear program

$$\min l+u$$

Subject to:

$$1p=1 \qquad\qquad (45)$$

Lower pi—l less than or equal to Ap less than or equal to upper pi +u

l, u, p greater than or equal to 0

(Jaumard et al. [117]), i.e., minimize the sum of enlargements of the probability intervals needed to restore satisfiability. As confidence in the (subjective) estimates of the various sentences may vary substantially, use can be made of the weighted objective function

$$\min w\overset{*}{l} + w\hat{u} \qquad\qquad (46)$$

where w and w are vectors of positive weights the larger the more the probability intervals (lower pi, upper pi) are considered to be accurate. Problem (45) and (46) can be solved by column generation algorithms, as discussed in Section 3, keeping the column corresponding to l and u explicit (or treating them separately as in the revised simplex algorithm).

While similar extensions of probability intervals for conditional probabilities might be considered the resulting problem would be a *bilinear program*, which is much more difficult to solve than a linear program."

Finally, in section 5.2, titled "Probabilistic Maximum Satisfiability", they show,

"A second way to restore satisfiability is to delete a subset of sentences with minimum cardinality (or possibly with minimum total weight, where weights of sentences are subjective estimates of their importance of reliability). This is done by solving . . . (a) mixed 0-1 linear program" (Hansen and Jaumard, 1996, pp. 40-42).

The only defect occurs in the conclusion of their paper:

"Probabilistic satisfiability and its extensions may be viewed as the applied, computation oriented (but including formal computing) side of probability logic, which is a very active research area. After a brilliant start, with Boole's work, followed by a long dormant period until Hailperin's first paper, it is now gaining impetus. Much work remains to be done, but the perspectives for theory and applications of probability satisfiability (including here the subjective probability approach of de Finetti and his school and its extension to imprecise probabilities by Walley) appear very promising." (Hanson and Jaumard, p. 51).

The insertion "with Boole's and Keynes' work" would make for a more accurate conclusion. It should also be mentioned that neither deFinetti nor Walley would support the use of the weighted objective function as they conflate degree of belief, degree of rational belief and degree of confidence in the probabilities, be they point, interval or ranked probabilities. Only Keynes' approach maintains a *clear* difference.

Thus, Keynes' ideas and the hard analysis with which he backed them lives on today in fuzzy logic, Boolean probability logic, AI and possibility theory. What is presented by Runde and Mizuhara, Meeks, Carabelli, O'Donnell, Fitzgibbons, Davis, Winslow, Dunn, etc., is a caricature of a genius. Only at the University of Cambridge are doctorate degrees awarded for analyzing Keynes' introductory diagram on page 39 of the TP.

2. The Origins and Logical Foundations of Keynes' Logical Theory of Probability and its Application: Major and Minor Figures.

> "Several modern writers have made some attempt at a symbolic treatment of probability. But with the exception of Boole, whose methods I have discussed in detail in Chapters 15, 16, and 17, no one has worked out anything very elaborate" (Keynes, 1921, p. 155).

The major figure is obviously George Boole. *Minor* figures would be Czuber, McColl, Johnson and Von Kries in that order. Nowhere in the TP does Keynes work out, expand, correct, and reapply any other author's work, except for Boole.

What about the logical foundations of Part V of the TP on statistics and statistical inference?

They major figures are Von Bortkiewicz, Lexis, Tchebycheff (Chebyshev) and Czuber. It is interesting that no economist has ever applied the Lexis Q test to time series data in order to answer the question Keynes put to Tinbergen in 1939 about the dynamic, intertemporal stability of Tinbergen's multiple regression equation. The answer, of course, would be that Tinbergen's equation system was *not* dynamically stable over time.

3. Conclusion—What can be done about the errors in Post Keynesian, Institutionalist and Cambridge (neo-Keynesian) Keynesian Thought?

The answer is that nothing can be done to correct errors that are so deeply entrenched and that have been passed on over the last 30 years, starting with Meeks in 1976. This section will simply repeat these errors so that future philosophers and historians of science can examine the psychological, emotional, mental and sociological framework that allowed these errors to be propagated through time with greater amplitude, frequency, and intensity.

Error 1—The foundation of Keynes' discussion of probabilistic measurement, non-comparability, incomplete or partial orderings, etc., is contained in Chapter III of the TP. Of great importance is the diagram on page 39 of the TP, 1921 (p. 42, 1973).

Error Correction—The foundation is contained in Chapters V, X, XV, XVI, and XVII of the TP. Chapter III is an introductory chapter similar of Chapter III of the GT. Nowhere in the TP or in any of Keynes' future work does he ever refer back to this diagram. In the GT, Chapter III is the introductory chapter. Chapters 19, 20 and 21, plus the appendix to Chapter 19, supply the actual mathematical analysis.

Error 2—Keynes gave three directly conflicting definitions of weight of evidence. This error was spread by Lawson and Runde.

Error Correction—Keynes gave three different *ways* in which weight of evidence can be *applied*. There is only one definition given by Keynes in the TP and that is,

$$0 \text{ less than or equal to } w \text{ less than or equal to } 1$$

where

$$w = K/(K+I)$$

and K and I have been normalized on the unit interval [0, 1] so that

0 less than or equal to K/(K+I)less than or equal to 1

and

wE[0,1].

Error 3—Von Kries is the source of Keynes' basic ideas on logical probability, non-numerical probability, and partial ordering. This nonsensical view derives from Fioretti and is supported by Lawson and Runde.

Error Correction—Anyone who is mathematically logically and statistically literate can read the relevant chapters of the TP and conclude, assuming they are rational, that George Boole is the original source and inspiration for Keynes. However, economists are famous for building sand castles in the sky. Anyway, Keynes' legacy is in good hands with Zadeh, Hailparin, Hansen and Jaumard, etc.

4. The End of the Myth of Keynes' "non-numerical" Probabilities.

Starting with the idiotic claims made by Frank Ramsey about Keynes' "non-numerical probabilities", in 1922 and 1926 through similar nonsense spread by Stohs (HOPE, 1980, 1983), Garner (HOPE 1983), Carabelli (1988), O'Donnell (1989), Lawson (EJ 1985, 1987), Runde (Econ. & Phil., 1990), Fioretti (Econ. And Phil., 2001; History. Econ. Ideas, 1998) and Weatherson (2002, Camb. J. Of Econ.), the following intellectual garbage has been allowed to circulate:

> "Keynes' theory of probability is based around some non-numerical values whose nature and behavior are left largely unexplained . . . hence the theory here, which captures the Keynesian intuitions while explaining away his mysterious non-numerical values . . . looks to be as good as it gets for a Keynesian theory of uncertainty" (Weatherson, 2002, p. 53, Camb. J. Of Econ.).

Weatherson's hilarious paper argues that Keynes' "intuitions" can be captured by interpreting Keynesian "non-numerical" probabilities as intervals. Of course, since Keynes spent three chapters of the TP, Chapters 15, 16, and 17 adapting Boole's approach into an interval estimate approach to probabilities and then used an extension of it (finite probabilities) as the foundation of Part III's TP analysis of analogy and induction, one must wonder what Weatherson was drinking and/or smoking when he wrote his paper? The same question can of course be asked of the editors and referees of the Cambridge Journal of Economics.

Footnotes

1   Thus, probabilities could be rational or irrational numbers for Boole and Keynes. Yet both types have rational upper and lower bounds, i.e., intervals.

2   There is a slight error in [maths.ucd.ie/rodgow/boole.pdf],

"In an analysis that seems much more modern in spirit than anything displayed by his contemporary workers in probability theory, Wilbraham shows that the solution to the problem is precisely what has been given above, and therefore the problem cannot be solved. Curiously, Keynes states: ' . . . Wilbraham gave as the solution $u = c_1 p_1 + c_2 p_2 - z$, where z is necessarily less than either $c_1 p_1$ or $c_2 p_2$. This solution is correct so far as it goes, but is not complete.' Here, u is just $p(E)$. In fact, Wilbraham says precisely what z is and his solution is complete. Keynes was well abreast of virtually all the literature on probability theory up to the end of the 19th Century, but he seems to have neglected to read Wilbraham's article in detail." The solution was,

"Now we have
$P(E) = p(E \text{ intersection } A_1 \text{ intersection } E \text{ intersection } A_2) = p(E \text{ intersection } A_1) + p(E \text{ intersection } A_2) - p(E \text{ intersection } A_1 \text{ intersection } A_2)$

$$=c_1p_1+c_2p_2-p(E \text{ intersection } A_1 \text{ intersection } A_2)$$

Since we have no information about the event E intersection A_1 intersection A_2, the problem is indeterminate." [Math ibid.]

[Math ibid] ignores Keynes' footnote 2 on page 167 of the TP:

"Boole's mistake was pointed out accurately though somewhat obscurely, by H. Wilbraham . . ." (Keynes, 1921, p. 167).

Keynes' objection is to the clearness of the exposition of Wilbraham, and not to "what z is".

Keynes, on page 188 of the TP, gives the following where

"$P(E \text{ intersection } A_1 \text{ intersection } A_2)$"

is expressed by Keynes as

"$ea_1a_2/h=y$,
$\qquad y=a_1a_2/eh\cdot e/h=uz$,
so that $u = (c_1p_1+c_2p_2)-y$."

This is identical to

"$p(E)= c_1p_1+c_2p_2-p(E \text{ intersection } A_1 \text{ intersection } A_2)$".

Further, Keynes gives an exhaustive analysis of all the other parts of Boole's problem. See TP, 1921, pages 188-189.

The reader should note that Keynes' criticisms of Boole's definition of "independence" (Keynes, 1921, pp 167-170; pp 186-188) are of a philosophical, epistemological and logical character, not mathematical or statistical. I agree with Keynes that Boole's first definition is correct. However, his second definition is inconsistent, vague, and ambiguous. From the *purely* statistical and mathematical point of view, Boole's operational definition, used in his problem solutions, is that the joint probability of two (or more) independent events is obtained by multiplying them together, i.e.,

$$P(A \text{ and } B) = P(A) \cdot P(B) \qquad (1)$$

or

$$P(A \text{ and } B \text{ and } C) = P(A) \, P(B) \, P(C), \text{ etc.}$$

Keynes states that "McColl . . . saw that Boole's fallacy turned on his *definition* of independence; but I do not think he understood, at least he does not explain, where precisely Boole's mistake lay." (Keynes, 1921 p. 167.) Similarly, neither Cayley or Wilbraham could point to a clear mathematical error. Instead of saying that Boole's first 6 problems in Chapter 20 of the laws of thought are "all erroneous", Keynes should have stated that they are problematic, vague, or ambiguous, i.e., assumptions are missing in the formulation of the problem. Of course, nowhere does Boole violate (1) in any of his problems. Again, note that a modified version of Boole's problem 10 serves as the foundation of Part III of the TP.

Given Boole's assumptions, his results are correct mathematically and statistically. Boole's *method*, although extremely difficult and unclear, is correct. The *assumptions* of what propositions are in fact independent and/or dependent therefore differs for Boole, McColl, Wilbraham, and Cayley. Thus, McColl's solution (identical to Wilbraham's) is, for

"$C_1 = 0.1$, $C_2 = 0.2$, $P_1 = 0.6$, $P_2 = 0.7$" [maths ibid, n.d. p 14]
equal to
"0.18 less than or equal to p(E) less than or equal to
0.186". [math ibid, n.d. p 14]

". . . Boole's solution is 0.190697319" (an irrational number) [math ibid, n.d., p 14].

Given the closeness of both numerical solutions, the dispute lies in the *first step*—what are the assumptions. Thus, there is no error in Boole's method or technique, given his assumptions. The error lies in his assumptions.

References

Adams, E.W. (1986). "On the Logic of High Probability", Journal of Philosophical Logic, 15, 255-79.

Anderson, K. and J. Hooker. (1994). "Bayesian Logic", Decision Support Systems, 11, 191-210.

Boole, G. (1854). An Investigation of the Laws of Thought . . . New York. Dover (reprint, 1958).

Chaines, A. and W. Cooper. (1962). "Programming in the Linear Fractional Functionals", Naval Research Logistics Quarterly, 9, 181-186.

Charniak, E. (1991). "Bayesian Networks Without Tears", AI Magazine, 12, 50-63.

Choquet, G. (1954). "Theory of Capacities", Annales de L'institut Fourier, 5, 131-291.

Hailperin, T. (1965). "Best Possible Inequalities for the Probability of a Logical Function of Events", American Mathematical Monthly, 72, 343-359.

Hailperin, T. (1976). Boole's Logic and Probability. Studies in logic and the foundations of mathematics, Vol, 85. North Holland: Amsterdam.

Hailperin, T. (1984). "Probability Logic", Notre Dame Journal of Formal Logic, 25, 198-212.

Hanson, P. and B. Jaumard. (1997). "Probabilistic Satisfiability". Unpublished paper.

Kampke, T. (1995). "Probabilistic Logic via Capacitie", International Journal of Intelligent Systems, 10, 857-869.

Keynes, J.M. (1921). A Treatise on Probability. London: MacMillan (1979 AMS reprinted).

Keynes, J.M. (1973). A Treatise on Probability. London: MacMillan. Volume VIII of collected works of John Maynard Keynes.

Lewis, D. (1976). "Probabilities of Conditionals and Conditional Probabilitics", Philosophical Review, 85, 297-315.

[Math ibid]. "George Boole and the Development of Probability Theory". In D. MacHale (?), (1985), George Boole. Dublin: Boole Press, 1-16.

Pan, Y. and B. Yuan. (1997). "Bayesian Inference of Fuzzy Probabilities", International Journal of General Systems, 26, 73-90.

Pearl, J. (1993). "Belief Networks Revisited", AI, 59, 49-56.

Runde, J. and S. Mizuhara. (2003). The Philosophy of Keynes' Economics: Probability, Uncertainty, and Convention. London: Routledge.

Sakawa, M. (1993). Fuzzy Sets and Interactive Multi Objective Optimisation. London: Plenum Press.

Smets, P. (1982). "Probability of a Fuzzy Event: an Axiomatic Approach", Fuzzy Sets and Systems, 7, 153-164.

Zadeh, L.A. (1965). "Fuzzy Sets", Information and Control, 8, 338-353.

Zadeh, L.A. (1978). "Fuzzy Sets as a Basis for a Theory of Possibility", Fuzzy Sets and Systems, 1, 3-28.

Zimmerman, H.J. (1985). Fuzzy Set Theory and Its Applications. Dordrecht: Kluwer Academic Publishers.

9

Keynesian Uncertainty, Ellsbergian Ambiguity, and Maxmin Expected Utility

A Comparison-Contrast

Abstract: A linear version of Keynes's non linear weighting function c gives numerical answers which are identical to those generated by Ellsberg's MMEU decision rule. The linearized, uncertainty averse version of Keynes's decision rule can easily be shown to be (a) a capacity (b) a belief function, and an (c)E-capacity subject to Dempster-Shafer Updating. The roles of ignorance and uncertainty (ambiguity) in Keynes's macroeconomic analysis of Involuntary Unemployment in his General Theory are related to his c coefficient model of 1921(1908)

1. Ellsberg's 1961 Three-color urn ball problem

Ellsberg specified the following problems in his 1961 article:

> "Another example yields a direct test of one of the Savage postulates. Imagine an urn known to contain 30 red balls and 60 black and yellow balls, the latter in unknown proportion. (Alternatively, imagine that a sample of two drawn from the 60 black and yellow balls has resulted in

one black and one yellow.) One ball is to be drawn at random from the urn; the following actions are considered:

	30 Red	Black	60 Yellow
I	$100	$0	$0
II	$0	$100	$0

Action I is "bet on red," II is "a bet on black." Which do you prefer?

Now consider the following two actions, under the same circumstances:

	30 Red	Black	60 Yellow
III	$100	$0	$100
IV	$0	$100	$100

Action III is a "bet on red or yellow"; IV is a "bet on black or yellow." Which of these do you prefer? Take your time!

A very frequent pattern of response is: action I preferred to II, and IV, preferred to III. Less frequent is: II preferred to I, and III preferred to IV. Both of these, of course, violate the Sure-thing Principle, which requires the ordering of I to II to be preserved in III and IV (since the two pairs differ only in their third column, constant for each pair)."[4] (Ellsberg, 1961, pp 653-654)

Ellsberg derived a decision rule aimed at dealing with the above problem:

"Assuming, purely for simplicity, that these factors enter into his decision rule in linear combination, we can denote by k (instead of Ellsberg's symbol rho) his degree of confidence, in a given state of information or ambiguity, in the estimated distribution y^e, which in turn reflects all of his judgments on the relative likelihood of distributions, including judgments of equal likelihood. Let $\min_x$ be the minimum expected pay-off to an act x as the probability distribution ranges over the set Y^0; let est_x be the expected pay-off to the act x corresponding to the estimated distribution y^e.

The simplest decision rule reflecting the above considerations would be *Associate with each x the Index:*

$$k \cdot \text{est}_x + (1\text{-}k) \cdot \min_x$$

Choose that act with the highest index.

In the case of the red, yellow and black balls, supposing no samples and no explicit information except that 1/3 of the balls are red, many subjects might lean toward an estimated distribution of (1/3, 1/3, 1/3): if not from "ignorance," then from counterbalancing considerations. But many of these would find the situation ambiguous; for them the "reasonable" distributions Y^0 might be all those between (1/3, 2/3, 0) and (1/3, 0, 2/3). Assuming for purposes of illustration $k = 1/4$ (Y^0, y^e, X and p are all subjective data to be inferred by an observer or supplied by the individual, depending on whether the criteria is being used descriptively or for convenient decision-making), the formula for the index would be:

$$1/4 \cdot \text{est}_x + 3/4 \min_x .$$

The relevant data (assigning arbitrary utility values of 6 and 0 to the money outcomes \$100 and \$0) would be:

	Red	Yellow	Black	Min_x	Est_x	Index
I	6	0	0	2	2	2
II	0	6	0	0	2	.5
III	6	0	6	2	4	2.5
IV	0	6	6	4	4	4

(Ellsberg, 1961, pp.664-665)

This decision rule was based on a decision rule formulated by Hodges-Lehman (1952).

Ellsberg also suggested an alternative decision rule:

> "An equivalent formulation would be the following, where y^0 is the estimated probability vector, y_x^{min} is the probability vector in Y^0 corresponding to min_x for action x and (X) is the vector payoffs for action x. *Associate with each x the index:*

$$[k . y^0 + (1\text{-}k) y_x^{min}] (x)$$

> *Choose that act with the highest index."*
>
> (Ellsberg, 1961, p.665)

> "In the equivalent formulation in terms of y_x^{min} and y^0, the subject above could be described "as though" he were assigning weights to the respective pay-offs of actions II and III, whose expected values are ambiguous, as follows (assuming $y^0 = (1/3, 1/3, 1/3)$ in each case):

	y_x^{min}	$k . y^0 + (1\text{-}k) y_x^{min}$
II	(1/3, 0, 2/3)	(1/3, 1/12, 7/12)
III	(1/3, 2/3, 0)	(1/3, 7/12, 1/12)

Although the final set of weights for each set of pay-offs resemble probabilities (they are positive, sum to unity, and represent a linear combination of two probability distributions), they differ for each action, since y_x^{min} will depend on the pay-offs for x and will vary for different actions. If these weights were interpreted as "probabilities," we would have to regard the subject's subjective probabilities as being dependent upon his pay-offs, his evaluation of the outcomes. Thus, this model would be appropriate to represent cases of true pessimism, or optimism or wishfulness (with y_x^{max} substituting for y_x^{min}). However, in this case we are assuming *conservatism*, not pessimism; our subject does not actually expect the worst, but he chooses to act *"as though" the worst were somewhat more likely than his best estimates of likelihood would indicate.* In either case, he violates the Savage axioms; it is impossible to infer from the resulting behavior a set of probabilities for *events* independent of his pay-offs. In effect, he "distorts" his best estimates of likelihood, in the direction of increased emphasis on the less favorable outcomes and to a degree depending on k, his confidence in his best estimate." (Ellsberg, p.667)

"Not only does this decision model account for "deviant" behavior in a particular, ambiguous situation, but it covers the observed shift in a subject's behavior as ambiguity decreases. Suppose that a sample is drawn from the urn, strengthening the confidence in the best estimates of likelihood, so that K increases, say, to 3/4. The weights for the pay-offs to actions II and III would now be:

$$k \cdot y^p + (1\text{-}k) \, y_x^{min}$$
$$\text{II } (1/3, 1/4, 5/12)$$
$$\text{III } (1/3, 5/12, 1/4)$$

and the over-all index would be: *Index*

I	2
II	1.5
III	3.5
IV	4

In other words, the relative influence of the consideration, "What is the worst to be expected?" upon the comparison of actions is lessened. The final weights approach closer to the "best estimate" values, and I and II approach closer to indifference, as do III and IV. This latter aspect might show up behaviorally in the amount a subject is willing to pay for a given bet on yellow, or on (red or black), in the two situations.

In the limit, as ambiguity diminishes for one reason or another and K approaches 1, the estimated distribution will come increasingly to dominate decision. With confidence in the best estimates high, behavior on the basis of the proposed decision rule will roughly conform to the Savage axioms, and it would be possible to infer the estimated probabilities from observed choices."(Ellsberg, p.668)

Ellsberg's formulation can be used by the 70-80% of individuals who make the "Ellsberg" choices, which are I P II and IV P III. This choice pattern violates SEU Theory, since, from I P II, one can derive the conclusion $PR>PB$., while from IV P III, one can derive the conclusion $P_B>P_R$. Behavior which is ambiguity averse is represented by the Ellsberg decision rules.

Ellsberg gives the following discussion of why ambiguity must be taken into account in decision making:

"A familiar, ongoing pattern of activity may be subject to considerable uncertainty, but this uncertainty is more apt to appear in the form of "risk"; the relation between given states of nature is known precisely, and although the random variation in the state of nature which "obtains" may be considerable, its stochastic properties are often known confidently and in detail. (Actually, this confidence may be self-deceptive, based on ignoring some treacherous possibilities; nevertheless, it commonly exists.) In contrast, the ambiguities surrounding the outcome of a proposed *innovation,* a departure from current strategy, may be much more noticeable. Different sorts of events are relevant to its outcome, and their likelihoods must now be estimated, often with little evidence or prior expertise; and the effect of a given state of nature upon the outcome of the new action may itself be in question. Its variance may not appear any higher than that of the familiar action when computed on the basis of "best estimates" of the probabilities involved, yet the meaningfulness of this calculation may be subject to doubt. The decision rule discussed will not preclude choosing such an act, but it will definitely bias the choice away from such ambiguous ventures and toward the strategy with "*known* risks." Thus the rule is "conservative" in a sense more familiar to everyday conversation than to statistical decision theory; it may often favor traditional or current strategies, even perhaps at high risk, over innovations whose consequences are undeniably ambiguous." (Ellsberg, 1961 p668-687)

2. Ellsberg's calculations:

The "best" estimate was given as P(red) P(yellow) P(black) equals (1/3, 1/3, 1/3). The other estimate chosen were (1/3, 2/3, 0) and (1/3, 0, 2/3). Obviously, there is an infinite number of other estimates *between* these limits. Given a degree of confidence of .25 (1/4), Ellsberg's results, using his *first* rule are, where the utility of \$100 = 6 and utility of \$0 = 0,

I—1/4 [1/3 (6)] + 3/4 [1/3 (6)] = 2.0 = EU.
II—1/4 [1/3 (6)] + 3/4 [0 (6)] = 1/2 = EU.
III—1/4 [1/3 (6) + 1/3 (6)] + 3/4 [1/3 (0)] = 2.5 = EU.
IV—1/4 [(4)] + 3/4 [(4)] = 4.0 = EU.

The results, using Ellsberg's second rule, where y^0 = (1/3, 1/3, 1/3), y_x^{min}, for II = (1/3, 0, 2/3) and y_x^{min}, for III = (1/3, 2/3, 0) are, for k = 1/4:

I   (1/3, _, _) ß (6,0,0) = 2.0 = EU.
II   1/4(1/3,1/3,1/3)+ 1(1/3,0,2/3)-1/4(1/3,0,2/3)
      = (1/12,1/12,1/12)+ (1/3,0,2/3)-(1/12,0,2/12)
      = [(1/12+1/3-1/12),(1/12+0-0),(1/12+2/3-2/12)]
      = (1/3,1/12,7/12). Then (1/3,1/12,7/12)ß(0,6,0)
      = .5 = EU.
III   1/4(1/3,1/3,1/3)+1(1/3,2/3,0)-1/4(1/3,2/3,0)
      = (1/12,1/12,1/12)+(1/3,2/3,0)-(1/12,0,2/12)

$$= [(1/12+1/3-1/12),(1/12+2/3-2/12),(1/12+0-0)]$$
$$= (1/3,7/12,1/12). \text{ Then } (1/3,7/12,1/12)ß(6,0,6)$$
$$= 2.5 = EU.$$

IV $$= [(1/3,1/3,1/3)]or(1/3,0,2/3)or(1/3,2/3,0)]ß(0,6,6)$$
$$= 4 = EU.$$

Later, Ellsberg postulates an increase in the degree of confidence which occurs, due to increased sampling. Now k = .75. Using Ellsberg's 2nd rule, we obtain

I $(1/3, \_, \_)$ ß $(6,0,0) = 2.0 = EU.$

II $3/4(1/3,1/3,1/3)+ 1(1/3,0,2/30)-3/4(1/3,0,2/3)$
$$= (3/12,3/12,3/12)+(1/3,0,2/3)-(3/12,0,6/12)$$
$$= [(3/12+1/3-3/12),(3/12+0+0),(3/12+2/3-6/12)\_$$
$$= (1/3,1/4,5/12). \text{ Then } (1/3,1/4,5/12)ß(0,6,0)$$
$$= 1.5 = EU.$$

III $3/4,(1/3,1/3,1/3)+1(1/3,2/3,0)-3/4(1/3,2/3,0)$
$$= (3/12,3/12,3/12)+(1/3,2/3,0)-(3/12,6/12,0)$$
$$= [(3/12,1/3,3/12), 3/12+2/3-6/12),(3/12+0+0)$$
$$= (1/3,5/12,1/4). \text{ Then } (1/3,5/12,1/4)ß(6,0,6)$$
$$= 3.5 = EU.$$

IV $$= [(1/3,1/3,1/3)]or(1/3,0,2/3)or(1/3,2/3,0)]ß(0,6,6)$$
$$= 4 = EU.$$

3. J.M. Keynes' analysis of 1921 (1908) and 1936

In chapter 26 of the *A Treatise on Probability* (TP), Keynes specified the following "conventional coefficient of risk and weight, where p + q = 1, 0 less than or equal to p, q less than or equal to 1, 0 less than or equal to w less than or equal to 1, for outcome A. For outcome A', p' + q' = 1, 0 less than or equal to p', q' less than or equal to 1 0 less than or equal to w' less than or equal to 1. This notation can be extended indefinitely, for example, for a Third possible outcome A", p" + q" = 1, 0 less than or equal to p", q" less than or equal to 1, 0 less than or equal to w" less than or equal to 1.

Keynes' rule is to Maximize cA, where

$$c = 2pw / [(1 + q) (1 + w)]$$

or

$$c = [p / (1 + q)] [2w / (1 + w)].$$

w is an index which measures the completeness of the relevant evidence or the amount of knowledge upon which the p's and q's are based. In the TP, Keynes' representation of this index is non-linear. Such an index is extremely important. For example, the standard decision Tree or Tree diagram representation of decision problems will give numerical answers that are inaccurate or unreliable unless w = 1.0. A w = 1.0 would specify the correct reference class. The 20 + years of controversy over the information content of the Tversky—Kahneman blue-green (or green-blue) Taxicab accident problem is precisely the result of ignoring Keynes' w index (see, for example, Koehler, J., 1996) in decision problems. Only urn ball problems, i.e., 100 balls in an urn, 85 green and 15 blue, have a w = 1.0

Ellsberg's representation of his k coefficient is linear. Following Ellsberg's specification, Keynes' w index is given a linear representation. We also eliminate the non-linear probability weighting factor $1/(1 + q)$, which deals with Allais type problems. Keynes's c coefficient is now

$$c = pw$$

as opposed to

$$c = p[2w / (1 + w)].$$

Given the small amount of money involved in Ellsberg's problems ($100), there will be no difference in answers using either EU or EV, since the utility functions will be linear.

As noted above, Keynes works with p and p'(w, w') in the generalized results given in footnote 2 on p.315 of the TP (1921). I note that the exact same formula and footnote appears in The

1908 Fellowship Thesis Version of the TP accepted by Cambridge University, England.

In the *General* Theory (GT), 1936, Keynes states, in chapter 3, that

> [3] "An entrepreneur, who has to reach a practical decision as to his scale of production does not, of course, entertain a single undoubting expectation of what the sale-proceeds of a given output will be, but several hypothetical expectations held with varying degrees of probability and definiteness. By his expectation of proceeds I mean, therefore, that expectations of proceeds which, if it were held with certainty, would lead to the same behaviour as does the bundle of vague and more various possibilities which actually makes up his state of expectation when he reaches his decision." (Keynes, GT, p.24 ft.3)

Later, in chapter 12, Keynes states that

> "It would be foolish, in forming our expectations, to attach great weight to matters which are very uncertain. [1] It is reasonable, therefore, to be guided to a considerable degree by the facts about which we feel somewhat confident, even though they may be less decisively relevant to the issue than other facts about which our knowledge is vague and scanty. For this reason the facts of the existing situation enter, in a sense disproportionately, into the formation of our long-term expectations; our usual practice being to take the existing situation and to project it into the future, modified only to the extent that we have more or less definite reasons for expecting a change.
>
> The state of long-term expectation, upon which our decisions are based, does not solely depend, therefore, on the probable forecast we can make. It also depends on the *confidence* with which we make this forecast—on how highly

we rate the likelihood of our best forecast turning our quite
wrong. If we expect large changes but are very uncertain as
to what precis form these changes will take, then our
confidence will be weak.

The *state of confidence*, as they term it, is a matter to
which practical men always pay the closest and most anxious
attention. But economists have not analysed it carefully and
have been content, as a rule, to discuss it in general terms."

[1] By "very uncertain" I do not mean the same thing as
"very improbable". *Cf.* my *Treatise on Probability,* chap. 6, on
"The Weight of Arguments". (Keynes, GT, pp. 148-149)

In both of these quotes, Keynes' use of the term "vague" has
the same meaning as Ellsberg's use of the term "ambiguity".
In chapter 17, Keynes states that

"The owners of wealth will then weigh the lack of
"liquidity" of different capital equipments in the above sense
as a medium in which to hold wealth against the best
available actuarial estimate of their prospective yields after
allowing for risk. The liquidity-premium, it will be observed,
is partly similar to the risk-premium, but partly different;—
the difference corresponding to the difference between the
best estimates we can make of probabilities and the
confidence with which we make them.[1] When we were
dealing, in earlier chapters, with the estimation of prospective
yield, we did not enter into detail as to how the estimation is
made: and to avoid complicating the argument, we did not
distinguish differences in liquidity from differences in risk
proper. It is evident, however, that in calculating the own-
rate of interest we must allow for both.

There is clearly, no absolute standard of "liquidity" but
merely a scale of liquidity—a varying premium of which
account has to be taken, in addition to the yield of use and
the carrying-costs, in estimating the comparative attractions

of holding different forms of wealth. The conception of what contributes to "liquidity" is a partly vague one, changing from time to time and depending on social practices and institutions. The order of preference in the minds of owners of wealth in which at any given time they express their feelings about liquidity is, however, definite and is all we require for our analysis of the behaviour of the economic system." (Keynes, GT, pp. 239-240)

The reader should note that *Both* Ellsberg and Keynes talk about a "best estimate" and "the other estimates", as well as the degree of confidence with which these estimates are held. Similarly, while Ellsberg emphasizes the role of confidence in dealing with *innovation*, Keynes emphasizes the role of confidence in long run investment decisions.

4. Keynes's numerical calculations

In this section, we use the linear w index plus Keynes's Principle of Indifference to obtain numerical answers for comparison with Ellsberg's approach.

We let $P_R = 1/3$, where the w of the red balls is $w_R = 1$. Similarly $P_Y = P_B = 1/3$ and $w_Y = w_B = 1/4$ for the yellow and black balls. Our goal is to

$$\text{maximize } c = pwA \text{ or } c = pwU(A).$$

For I, EU (EV) = $(1/3)(1)(6)+(1/3)(1/4)(0)+(1/3)(1/4)(0) = 2.0$
For II, EU = $(1/3)(1)(0)+(1/3)(1/4)(6)+(1/3)(1/4)(0) = 0.5$
For III, EU = $(1/3)(1)(6)+(1/3)(1/4)(0)+(1/3)(1/4)(6) = 2.5$
For IV, EU = $(1/3)(1)(0)+(1/3)(1)(6)+(1/3)(1)(6) = 4.0$

Now let us take Keynes's w index and integrate it into the Hodges-Lehman approach adapted by Ellsberg to model his concerns about the ambiguity of information and the confidence a

decision maker has in his analysis. We use w ß est$_x$ + (1-w) · min x
and pick the highest index.

The exact same answers will be obtained as presented in Section
2 above.

Now incorporate Keynes' w index into Ellsberg's second
suggested decision rule. We obtain

$$[w \text{ ß } y^0 + (1\text{-}w) \, y_x^{min}] \, x$$

and choose the highest index. Again, we obtain exactly the same
precise answers worked out in section 2 above.

Now vary the degree of confidence w and let it equal $w_Y = w_B =$
.75 for yellow and black balls. For red balls, $w_R = 1.0$. Again, using
Keynes's Principle of Indifference, the probabilities for the red,
black, and yellow balls are $P_R = P_B = P_Y = 1/3$.

For I
    EU = (1/3)(1)(6)+(1/3)(3/4)(0)+(1/3)(3/4)(0) = 2.0.
For II
    EU = (1/3)(1)(0)+(1/3)(3/4)(6)+(1/3)(3/4)(0) = 1.5.
For III
    EU = (1/3)(1)(6)+(1/3)(3/4)(0)+(1/3)(3/4)(6) = 2+(1/4)(6)
        = 2 + 1.5 = 3.5.
For IV
    EU = (1/3)(1)(0)+(1/3)(1)(6)+(1/3)(1)(6) = 4.0

We obtain the exact same set of answers as Ellsberg did. Now
use a w = .75 as in Ellsberg's second decision rule. The exact same
answers would result as given in section II above.

Both Keynes and Ellsberg are talking about and analyzing the
same problem. Given that the dates of Keynes' contributions are 1908,
1921, and 1936, while Ellsberg's in 1961, it is a shame that Keynes's
Technical analysis of decision-making using his conventional coefficient
approach, has been overlooked in the literature, the exception being
the author of this paper, on decision-making in the 20th Century.

5. E-capacities

In Eichberger and Kelsey, 1999, it is shown that Ellsberg's ambiguity averse representation is a capacity, a belief function, an E-capacity, and for a linear *k*, the Choquet integral of an E-capacity is identical to Ellsberg's decision rule. Further,

> "E-capacities are belief functions and updating them by the Dempster-Shafer rule corresponds to updating according to the maximum likelihood principle. Dempster-Shafer updating guarantees already that the updated preferences can be represented again by a Choquet integral. We will show however that the Dempster-Shafer update of an E-capacity is itself an E-capacity. This is a particularly useful property in economic applications." (Eichberger and Kelsey, 1999, p.128)

However, *all* of the Eichberger-Kelsey results hold for Keynes' w coefficient if we give Keynes' degree "of the completeness of the evidence" or "most complete knowledge" (TP, 1921, p.315) a linear representation instead of the non-linear representation Keynes specified nearly a century (1908) ago. A linear formulation of Keynes's weighting index w, within the Hodges Lehman rule adopted for use by Ellsberg, is the Choquet integral. All the results obtained by Eichburger and Kelsey using Ellberg's formulation are duplicated exactly if one instead substitutes Keynes's formulation.

6. A Thought Experiment

Let us suppose that Ellsberg was *not* ignorant of Keynes' s contributions of 1921 and 1936. Suppose that Ellsberg had come across Keynes' *TP* and *GT* some time in the mid 1950's and decided to use the linear modified version of Keynes' conventional coefficient of risk and weight, used in section 4 above, in order to operationalize his criticisms of Savages SEU theory, instead of the Hodges-Lehman approach (1952). Given these two suppositions, we can ask the following question. Would *any* of Ellsberg's arithmetic results or conclusions have differed from the published paper's arithmetic results or conclusions? The answer, of course, is no, except that Ellsberg emphasized the ambiguity of *innovation*, whereas Keynes emphasized the *Uncertainty* of *long run investment*.

A second question follows from the first. What is new, original, innovative, creative, or novel *at the Theoretical level*, in Ellsberg's work, that represents an improvement over Keynes's representation? The answer, of course, is that there is no new Theoretical development in Ellsberg's paper compared to Keynes's *Theoretical* analysis in the *TP*

Keynes's major points were that the EV (EMV) approach, even if modified by a Bernoulli Utility function, ignored non linear probability preferences (Keynes, 1921, p.313) and the weight of the evidence (the vagueness and/or uncertainty of the GT). EV is thus a special, Limiting case only of a more general approach.

Ellsberg's major point was that Savages' SEU approach ignored ambiguity. SEU is a special, limiting case. Ellsberg's contribution is thus an *applied* and quasi-*experimental* one. Ellsberg's two problems allow the reader to clearly see that the Savage SEU approach *is* a limiting case only. Ellsberg's problems specification is thus clearly superior to the purely theoretical, generalized solution forms given by Keynes in the TP in chapter 26 on p.315 in footnote 2 or in chapter 30.

We are then led to a third and final question. Why have Keynes's technical, theoretical contributions been *totally* ignored for so many years? Possibly this is due to the post WWII craze for axiomatic foundations. According to this view, a rational decision maker should not use aspirin to relieve a headache unless he has a completely specified mathematical and statistical model explaining precisely the physio-chemical transmission mechanisms in the brain that eliminate the headache, as well as a statistical test at the .10 level of significance that does not reject the null hypothesis that aspirin works, followed by cross-sectional (point in time) and time series (over time) or panel data evidence that forecasts headache relief accurately. Perhaps a more pragmatic justification is in order that would support the use of Keynes' c coefficient. *It works.* Or one might provisionally adopt the Eichberger-Kelsey axiomatic construct used to support Ellsberg's representation to also support Keynes's representation. The objections that Ellsberg discussed concerning SEU are practically the same as the objections Keynes raised about EMV.

It is time, from a history of decision making perspective, to give Keynes his due. This has not been the case in economics, as Keynes's involuntary unemployment category rests heavily on the existence of ambiguity in long run decisions to invest (or not invest and hold money or other highly liquid financial assets like stocks, bonds, indexes, derivatives, commodity future contracts, etc., instead). This problem does not occur if the exact probability distribution is well defined. This is the case of risk that the Savage axioms exemplify and which non-Keynesian economists accept. Under linear risk, involuntary unemployment is not a problem. Under conditions of ignorance ($k = 0$) or uncertainty ($k < 1$), conventional classical and neoclassical maxims about rational economic behavior collapse. Only under conditions of linear risk and certainty, the limiting cases for both Ellsberg and Keynes, does the "rational" economic optimizer approach lead to both valid and sound theory and practice in the classical/neoclassical sense. R. Lucas, Jr., speaking for the classical and neoclassical schools, admits this. Thus, "In cases of uncertainty, economic reasoning will be of no value", since business cycles must be "repeated instances of essentially similar events". (Lucas, 1977, p. 15. See also Lucas, 1981, p. 223-224 and 273-274).

7. Keynes and Indeterminate Probabilities

Keynes was the *first* decision theorist to introduce the concepts of "interval estimates" and/or "numerically indeterminate probabilities", as well as non-comparability, which arises when intervals overlap. In chapters 15 and 17 of the TP, he develops

Boole's approach into a mathematically demanding way of calculating upper-lower limits, bounds, or probabilities, assuming linearity. (Keynes, 1921, p. 163). A good summary of Keynes's position is on p.373 (Keynes, 1921, p. 373).

"What . . . does Laplace mean by an unknown probability? . . . he seems to apply the term to any probability whose value, according to the argument of chapter III., is numerically indeterminate (author's emphasis). Thus he assumes that every probability has a numerical value . . where there seems to be no numerical value . . . where the numerical value is unknown . . . every value between 0 and 1 is equally probable. With the possible interpretations of the term 'unknown probability', and with the theory that every probability can be measured by *one* (author's emphasis) of the real numbers between 0 and 1, I have dealt, as carefully as I can., in chapter III".

Thus,

"It is assumed . . . that the number of possible sets of antecedent conditions is proportional to the numbers of real numbers between 0 and 1; and that these fall into equal groups, each group corresponding to *one* of the real numbers between 0 and 1, this number measuring the degree of probability." (Keynes, 1921, pp 374-375; authors' underscore). The same argument appears on p.237. Keynes states

"I argued in chapter III, that not all probabilities have an exact numerical value . . . there is one class of probabilities . . . which I called the numerical class, the ratio of each of whose numbers to certainty can be expressed by *some number less than unity*; (authors' underscore) and we can sometimes compare a non-numerical probability in respect of more and less, with one of these numerical probabilities. This enables us to give a definition of 'finite probability' *which is capable of application* to *non-numerical* (authors' underscore) as well as to numerical probabilities. I define a 'finite probability' as one which exceeds some numerical probability, the ratio of which to certainty can be expressed by a finite number". (Keynes, TP, 237)

Thus, by "non-numerical" Keynes means "not by a single numeral". Keynes made a heroic intellectual effort to axiomatize *both* "numerical" and "non-numerical" probabilities in chapters 12-14 of the TP. In chapter 15, he presents the set of axioms that would deal with numerical probabilities only. In chapter 8, he presents the set of axioms needed for a relative frequency interpretation. It is clear that all of the above went over F.P. Ramsey's head. The result was Ramsey's claim that all probabilities can be represented by a unique, additive, single number, ie. Laplace's error. Note that Keynes' view on indeterminate probabilities did not alter. In 1935, in response to a query from Ralph Hawtrey about Effective Demand, Keynes states:

> 6. *Effective demand.* The process here is exactly the same as that by which a market price is fixed for a share of which no one really knows the prospective yield accurately. I was really conceding too much in saying that it was a fiction. The market is regularly engaged in assessing, in terms of an exact numeral, a complex of rather vague probabilities. (Keynes, CWJMK, Vol.13, p 632)

8. Keynes's c coefficient and the MMEU decision rule.

A linear version of Keynes's c coefficient gives the exact same numerical answers as the MMEU decision rule covered by Ellsberg, Gardenfors, Gardenfors and Sahlin, Gilboa, Schmeidler, Gilboa and Schmeidler, Kelsey, and Sarin and Wakker (see references). However, Keynes's rule does not require any maxmin assumption, is easier to use, apply and understand, and is simpler. Using Occam's Razor as a guide, Keynes 1921 rule (1908) is thus preferable as a decision rule. Keynes's rule is also more general, as Keynes's formulation is specifically non-linear. The above referenced authors all *assume* linearity in their weighting functions. None of the various axiomatic version of MMEU hold for non-linear decision weights.

9. Conclusions

Keynes concluded that uncertainty (ambiguity), non-linear risk, and ignorance were of fundamental importance in explaining the existence of involuntary unemployment. Involuntary Unemployment can't exist in decision making under certainty and linear risk, as for instance, exemplified in Lucas's reinterpretation of Khinchin's gas particle model as a macroeconomic model where large, identical consumer-producer populations are analyzed as if they were large populations of gas particles subject to the law of large numbers and Central Limit Theorem (see Lucas, 1981, 120-124, 206-209, 223-224, 284-286). Lucas is forced to deny the appicability of decision making under ignorance, uncertainty, or non linear risk due to the *particular mathematical formulation* of his model.

At the macroscopic level, the linear risk formulation of EV, EMV, EU, and SEU will lead to the conclusion that the average, or mean, position of the private sector economy is on the boundary of its production possibilities frontier. Only mild, minor inventory recession or inflations are possible in such a world. On the other hand, decision rules such as Keynes's c coefficient or MMEU will result in expected values or returns that represent interior positions for private sector economies subject to ignorance, uncertainty (ambiguity), or non linear risk. The larger the difference between a SEU analysis and a MMEU analysis, the greater the amount of Involuntary Unemployment that will exist.

Keynes attacked the Benthamite Utilitarian rule of maximizing the expected value (EV) or expected monetary value (EMV) because it ignored the completeness of the evidence (w) and non-linear probability preferences. In its place, Keynes suggested the use of what I have renamed a weighted monetary value rule (WMV). In a very similar fashion, Ellsberg attacked the Savage rule of maximizing expected Utility (EU) or subjective expected utility (SEU) because it ignored the ambiguity and/or vagueness of the evidence (k). In its place, Ellsberg suggested maximizing a weighted minimum expected utility (WMEU). This approach, with appropriate axiomatic foundations, was called Max Min Expected Utility (MMEU). This approach is certainly superior to SEU. However, I believe that this paper presents sufficient evidence that a modified c coefficient is superior to MMEU from an applied point of view.

Footnote

[1]   Use of Keynes' non-linear formulation will result in slightly different numerical answers, but give the same ordinal ranking. Thus $2(.25)/(1 + .25) = .40$.

We obtain the following results:

I-EU = $(1/3)(1)(6)+(1/3)(2/5)(0)+(1/3)(2/5)(0) = 2.0$
II-EU = $(1/3)(1)(0)+(1/3)(2/5)(6)+(1/3)(2/5)(0) = 0.8$
III-EU = $(1/3)(1)(6)+(1/3)(2/5)(0)+(1/3)(2/5)(6) = 2.8$
IV-EU = $(1/3)(1)(0)+(1/3)(1)(6)+(1/3)(1)(6) = 4.0$

For a K (w) = .75, $2(.75)/(1 + .75) = .857$, we obtain the following results:

I-EU = $(1/3)(1)(6)+(1/3)(.857)(0)+(1/3)(.857)(0) = 2.0$
II-EU = $(1/3)(1)(0)+(1/3)(.857)(6)+(1/3)(.857)(0) = 1.71$
III-EU = $(1/3)(1)(6)+(1/3)(.857)(0)+(1/3)(.857)(6) = 3.71$
IV-EU = $(1/3)(1)(0)+(1/3)(1)(6)+(1/3)(1)(6) = 4.0$

In order to obtain these results from Keynes's original formulation, with either a linear or non-linear w, no additional assumption was introduced. Eichberger and Kelsey, and Ellsberg implicitly, have introduced the MMEU criterion, max min expected utility. Schmeidler also adds MMEU, as do a host of other decision theorists whose works are not referenced in this paper. Based on Occam's Razor, Keynes' approach is simpler and more general.

References

Brady, M.E. (1987), "J.M. Keynes'" Theory of Evidential Weight":
   It's Relation to Information Processing Theory and Application
   in the General Theory", Synthese, 71, 37-59.
Brady, M.E. (1993), "J.M. Keynes' Theoretical Approach to
   Decision Making under Conditions of Risk and Uncertainty",
   British Journal for the Philosophy of Science, 43, 357-376.
Brady, M.E. (1994), "On the Application of Keynes' Approach to
   Decision Making", International Studies in the Philosophy
   of Science, 8, 99-112.
Brady, M.E. (1994) "J.M. Keynes' Decision Theory: A Technical
   Note", Psychological Reports, 74, 465-66.
Brady, M.E. (1994), "A Note on the Extension of J.M. Keynes'
   Decision Theory", Psychological Reports, 75, 112-114.
Brady, M.E. (1997), "Decision Making under Uncertainty in
   the A Treatise on Probability: Keynes' Mathematical
   solution of the 1961 Ellsberg Two Color Ambiguous Urn
   Ball Problem in 1921", History of Economics Review, 26,
   136-142.
Brady, M.E. (2000), "J.M. Keynes' Decision Theory and Preference
   Reversals", International Journal of Applied Economics and
   Econometrics", In Press.
Brady, M.E. (2000), "Further Applications of J.M. Keynes'
   Approach to Decision Making under Risk and Uncertainty",
   International Journal of Applied Economics and
   Econometrics", In Press.
Brady, M.E. and Lee, H.B. (1989), "Is There an Ellsberg-Fellnes
   Paradox? A Note on its Resolution", Psychological Reports,
   64, 1087-90.
Casadesus-Masanell, R. Klibanoff, P. and Ozdenoren, E. (2000)."
   Maxmin expected utility through statewise combinations",
   Economic Letters, 66, pp.49-54.
Chi, T. and Fan, D. (1997), "Cognitive Limitations and
   Investment" 'Myopia'," Decision Sciences, 28, 27-51.

Currie, M. and Kubin, I. (1992), "Investment in Fixed Capital and Competitive Industry Dynamics", Oxford Economic Papers, 49, 521-542.

Eichberger, J. and Kelsey, D. (1999), "E-Capacities and the Ellsberg Paradox", Theory and Decision, 46, 107-140.

Ellsberg, D. (1961), "Risk, Ambiguity, and the Savage Axioms," Quarterly Journal of Economics, 75, 643-669.

Fishburn, P.C. (1991). "On the Theory of Ambiguity" International Journal of Information and Management Science, 2, pp. 1-16.

Gardenfors, P. (1979). "Forecasts, Decisions and Uncertain Probabilities", Erkenntnis, 14, pp. 159-181.

Gardenfors, P. and Sahlin, N-E. (1982). "Unreliable Probabilities, Risktaking and Decision Making," Synthese, 53, pp. 361-386.

Gardenfors, P. and Sahlin, N.E. (1983). "Decision Making with Unreliable Probabilities", British Journal of Mathematical and Statistical Psychology, 36, pp. 240-251.

Gilboa, I. (1987). "Expected Utility with Purely Subjective Non-additive Probabilities, Journal of Mathematical Economics, 16, pp. 65-88.

Gilboa, I. (1988). "A Combination of Expected Utility Theory and Maxmin Decision Criteria", Journal of Mathematical Psychology, 32, pp. 405-420.

Gilboa, I. and Schmeidler, D. (1989). "Maxmin Expected Utility with a Non-Unique Prior", Journal of Mathematical Economics, 18, pp. 141-153.

Guiso, L. and Parigi, G. (1999), "Investment and Demand Uncertainty", Quarterly Journal of Economics, 185-227.

Hodges, Jr., J.L. and Lehman, E.L., (1952), "The Uses of Previous Experiences in Reaching Statistical Decision", Annals of Mathematical Statistics, 23, 396-407.

Kelsey, D. (1995). "Dutch Books Argument and Learning in a Non Expected Utility Framework", International Economic Review, 36, pp. 187-206.

Kelsey, D. (1994). "Max Min Expected Utility and Weight of Evidence", Oxford Economic Papers, 46, pp. 425-444.

Kelsey, D. (1993). "Choice Under Partial Uncertainty", International Economic Review, 34, pp. 297-308.

Keynes, J.M. (1921). A Treatise on Probability. Macmillan, England.

Keynes, J.M. (1964). The General Theory of Employment, Interest and Money. Harcourt, Brace, and Company, New York.

Koehler, J.J. (1996). "The base rate fallacy reconsidered: Descriptive, Normative, and methodologcial challenges", Behavioral and Brain Sciences, 19, pp 1-53.

Levi, I. (1985). "Imprecision and Indeterminacy in Probability Judgement", Philosophy of Science, 52, pp. 390-409.

Levi, I. (1974). "On Indeterminate Probabilities", The Journal of Philosophy, pp 391-410.

Lucas, R.E., Jr (1977), "Understanding Business Cycles", Journal of Monetary Economics Supplement, Carnegie-Rochester Conference Series, Vol. 5.

Lucas, R.E., Jr (1981), "Methods and Problems in Business Cycle Theory". In Studies in Business Cycle Theory. MIT Press, USA.

Sarin, R. and Wakker, P. (1992). "A Simple Axiomatization of Nonadditive Expected Utility", Econometrics, 60, pp 1255-1273.

10

A Comparison-Contrast Between Keynes' *A Treatise on Probability* (1921) and Ellsberg's *Risk, Ambiguity and Decision*(2001) on Partial Orders, Interval Estimates, Upper and Lower Probabilities, Non-linear Decision Weights, Vague or Ambiguous Urnball Models, Degrees of Confidence, Decision Rules and Indeterminate Probabilities

Abstract— A careful reading of the *entire A Treatise on Probability* (1921) demonstrates that Keynes had systematically developed a formal apparatus for constructing what "modern" decision theorists label as "partial orders, interval estimates, upper and lower probabilities, indeterminate probabilities, vagueness or ambiguity, degrees of confidence, non-linear decision weights, non-additive probabilities", etc. Thus, *with respect to Keynes' work*, there is practically nothing in Ellsberg's *Risk, Ambiguity and Decision* (2001) which is new, original, novel, innovative, or inventive. Of course, compared to Koopman, Good and Savage, Ellsberg's work is a breakthrough.

1. Introduction

E llsberg, in his discussions of J.M. Keynes' *Treatise on Probability* (1921), in his dissertation, recently published in 2001 as *Risk, Ambiguity and Decision*, reveals a very deep understanding of the small portion of the TP that he read. This partial reading of the TP consists of Chapter 3, 6, and section 7 of Chapter 26 (Ellsberg, pp. 8-14, 91-97, 100, 110, 123, and 193). Based on this partial reading, Ellsberg does quite well. He realizes that Keynes' probability logic is one of partial orders or entailment, that Keynes clearly distinguishes between probability and weight (weight of arguments), that Keynes introduced non-comparability of beliefs and that such an approach is fully rational.

Unfortunately, Ellsberg leaves out vast amounts of Keynes' formal analysis which Keynes adopted from George Boole. The rest of the paper catalogs the huge gaps in Ellsberg's understanding. Having said this, I conclude that Ellsberg's discussion of Keynes, incomplete as it is, is vastly superior to the much more recent hodgepodge of ignorant commentaries made by Paul Davidson, Tony Lawson, Jochen Runde, Guido Fioretti, Anna Carabelli, Rod O'Donnell, Gay Meeks, Athol Fitzgibbons, Bradley Bateman, etc., ad nauseum.

2. Keynes and Boole

First, laying the ground work in Chapters 5 and 10 of the TP, Keynes adopts Boole's 1854 *Laws of Thought* approach to specifying upper and lower probability limits or bounds as well as allowing both rational and irrational numbers to represent the probability relation. This is done in Chapters 15, 16, and 17 of the *TP*. This is all that needs to be said. Hailparin (1965) made the breakthrough, showing how all of Boole's (and hence Keynes') problems could be reworked using linear programming, integer programming, the simplex method, etc. When Ellsberg discusses "upper and lower intuitive probabilities" (in the Koopman/Good sense) (Ellsberg, 2001, pp. 173-174, pp. 113-124, Chapter III, Appendix to Chapter III), he leaves a giant black hole by not discussing Keynes' approach, an approach that Keynes makes, in terms of his definition of "finite probability" the foundation for his entire discussion of analogy in Part III of the TP.

Unfortunatey, Keynes called his intervals (lower and upper probability limits) "non numerical", by which Keynes meant "not by a single number", but by *two* numbers. A large number of articles in economics journals talk about Keynes' "mysterious", "unfathomable", "what is a non numerical probability?" approach. The most recent is Weatherson's 2001 Cambridge Journal of Economics article.

3. Ellsberg's (2001)—An assessment of his understanding of the *TP*'s decision criteria.

Ellsberg's (Levi, 2001, pp. XIX-XX and Ellsberg, 2001, pp. 131-137) two color ambiguous urn problem is identical to the example discussed by Keynes in Chapter 6 of the *TP*. We know Ellsberg read Chapter 6 of the *TP*. Yet, there is no discussion of Keynes' urn example anywhere in either the 1961 QJE articles, in Ellsberg (2001), or in Levi (2001). This author wants to know why.

4. Ellsberg (2001)—Continued.

Ellsberg states:

> "But *how* does it depend? How may the web of action systematically reflect the varying degrees of "vagueness" of "ambiguity/weight," of "confidence" in our judgment? On that question, which is of central interest in this study, Knight is virtually silent, as are Savage and Keynes (Good makes several conjectures, identical to some examined in Chapters Six and Seven). It is a puzzle, they agree.[2] Knight offers the comment" "The ultimate logic, or psychology, of these deliberations is obscure, a part of the scientifically unfathomable mystery of life and mind."[3] But where the recent "neo-Bernoullians" tend to shrug their shoulders at

the difficulties of expressing these factors and measuring
their influence, effectively ignoring them in their formal
theorizing, Keynes, like Knight, emphasizes that these
matters do seem relevant to decision-making, though
admitting frankly his own vagueness and lack of confidence
on this particular question:

> In deciding on a course of action, it seems plausible
> to suppose that we ought to take account of the weight
> as well as the probability of different expectations. But
> it is difficult to think of any clear example of this, and
> I do not feel sure that the theory of 'evidential weight'
> has much practical significance.[4]
>
> If two probabilities are equal in degree, ought we,
> in choosing our course of action, to prefer that one
> which is based on a greater body of knowledge?
>
> The question appears to me to be highly
> perplexing, and it is difficult to say much that is useful
> about it. But the degree of completeness of the
> information upon which a probability is based does
> seem to be relevant, as well as the actual magnitude of
> the probability, in making practical decisions . . . If, for
> one alternative, the available information is necessarily
> small, that does not seem to be a consideration which
> ought to be left out of account altogether.[1]

When John Maynard Keynes expresses himself with so much
diffidence on a subject, it is, perhaps, excusable when later theorists
shy from committing themselves upon it and make some effort to
build theories on other foundations; but it seems incautious of
them to try to ignore that subject entirely. In Chapter Five I shall
argue, and propose some evidence, that theories that do so are for
that reason inadequate. In Chapters Six and Seven I shall examine
a number of decision criteria, and support several, that give formal
roles to factors that may plausibly be identified with the concepts

---

[1]   *Ibid.,* p. 313.

of "vagueness", "ambiguity" and "confidence" discussed above and that imply systematic influence by these variables upon decision-making: influence of a sort that is ignored (indeed, ruled out as "unreasonable"—a judgment I shall challenge) by the "neo-Bernoullian" decision theorists.

Thus, I regard as premature the resignation expressed by L. J. Savage:

> Some people see the vagueness phenomenon as an objection; I see it as a truth, sometimes unpleasant but not curable by a new theory.[2]

Though inspired by my own sense of the current inadequacies of the neo-Bayesian approach, the present work may be interpreted as a direct response to the challenge implicit in the last quotation above. I accept fully the point of view of personal probability as being "nothing else than the expression of beliefs about unknown facts"[3], but I am impressed by the fact that any single, definite probability distribution seems a profoundly *bad* expression of vague, semi-formed beliefs in situations of extreme ambiguity.[4]

Of course, Keynes did give a formal role to the "ambiguity" factor. Unfortunately, Ellsberg, like Levi, Lawson, Runde, and a host of other economists, never got to page 315 of the *TP*, contained in Section 8 of Chapter 26. Of course, the footnote on page 76 of Chapter 6 of the TP asks the reader to read Section 7 of Chapter 26. Section 8 contains Keynes' formal specification of an index to measure weight of evidence, the formal specification of his conventional coefficient of risk and weight, C, as well as the *general* solution to *all* of the problems consdered

---

2   Savage, "Bayesian Statistics", lecture at the Third Symposium on Decision and Information Processes, April, 1961, to be published in *Decision and Information Processes,* Macmillan.

[4]*Op. Cit.,* P. 76. Keynes is equally apologetic in introducing his chapter on "The Weight of Arguments": "The question to be raised in this chapter is somewhat novel; after much consideration I remain uncertain as to how much importance to attach to it." (*Ibid.,* p. 71.)" (Ellsberg, 2001, pp. 13-14).

in Ellsberg's book, including the n-color problem and the Allais problem contained in footnote 2 on page 315 of the *TP*. Keynes' analysis is contained on page 315. A complete *mathematical* analysis of the two color problem is made by Keynes in Chapter 30 of the *TP*. With respect to Keynes, Ellsberg's Chapters 5, 6, and 7 are redundant.[1] Thus, Ellsberg's claims that,

> "[1]Keynes and Koopman do not commit themselves as to the impact of "vagueness" upon decision-making. Good has some highly pertinent comments, discussed below, that are consistent with these assertions." (Ellsberg, p. 97).

and,

> "Many writers, including Frank Knight and Lord Keynes, have insisted upon the feasibility and relevance of this sort of judgment, without indicating precisely how it might affect decision-making; we shall consider now a meaningful role." (Ellsberg, 193)

are simply false when directed at Keynes. Ellsberg is correct in his evaluation of Knight and Good. Similarly, Machina (2001) claims that,

> "The appearance of Ellsberg's classic 1961 article posed such a challenge to accepted theories of decision making that, after an some initial rounds of discussion,[1] the issues he raised remained well-known but largely unaddressed, simply because researchers at the time were helpless to address them. It took more than a quarter of a century, and the successful resolution of separate issues raised by Allais (1953), before decision scientists were in a position to take on the deeper issues raised by the Ellsbreg Paradox." (Machina, 2001, p. XXXIX)

is also false. Keynes' coefficient analysis in 1907, 1908, and 1921 solves all of the problems considered by Ellsberg (2001) in his book.

Finally, Ellsberg's rho, defined as

"a number between 0 and 1 reflecting the decision-maker's degree of confidence in or reliance upon the estimated distribution y^0 in a particular decision problem." (Ellsberg, 2001, p. 194)

is practically the same as Keynes' w, wE[0, 1], defined by Keynes on page 315 of the *TP*.

5. Non-linear decision weights and/or non-or-sub (super) additive probabilities (capacities).

Keynes' coefficients can be sub-proportional (sub-additive) and super-proportional (super-additive) depending on the non-linear weighting factors $[1/(1+q)]$ and $[2w/(1+w)]$. If one uses w instead of $[2w/(1+w)]$ then one obtains Ellsberg's special case of a *linear* weighting function.

Kampke (1995) demonstrated that the Choquet capacities approach is a special case of Boolean probabilistic logic. One simply changes the linear programming problems inequality constraint, in the standard probabilistic logic approach, from

$$\_p = 1$$
$$Ap = pi$$
$$p \text{ greater than or equal to } 0$$

to

$$\_p_i = 1 \quad i = 1, 2, \ldots, n$$
$$A \min (p_1, p_2, \ldots p_n) = "$$
$$p_i \text{ greater than or equal to } 0 \quad i = 1, 2 \ldots, n$$

Thus, the lower probability is the minimum probability distribution from the set of probability distributions $(p_1 \ldots p_n)$.

Given that Boole, based on Keynes' shrewd and brilliant reinterpretation of his approach, established the entire concept of upper and lower probabilities, Kampke's result should not come as a surprise. The same result holds for the work of C.A.B. Smith, H. Kyburg, Jr., Koopmans, both I.J. Goods, Levi, Dempster, Shafer, Dempster-Shafer, Gilboa, Schmeidler, Gilboa-Schmeidler, Fishburn, etc., etc., etc., all of their lower-upper probability approaches or convex-concave capacities can be shown to be special cases of Boole's original analysis.

6. Conclusion

Given that Parts I-IV of the *TP* (1921) are practically identical to the 1907 and 1908 Cambridge Fellowship theses, one can trace Keynes' analytic *formal* understanding of the effects of decision-making under conditions of risk, uncertainty (ambiguity) and ignorance, as they relate to the study of investment and speculation in the world's stock markets, back to those years. Keynes had a complete *formal* model of decision making to support his literary discussions. Thus, the Ramsey-DeFinette-Von Neumann and Morgenstern-Savage models, are, like the Benthamite Utilitarian model, special cases of Keynes' *model*.

Footnotes

[1]   There is one area of decision theory where Ellsberg is, in a formal modeling sense, ahead of Keynes.

   Ellsberg incorporates his degree of confidence index, rho, rho E[0,1] into the Hurwicz rule, which measures optimism (overconfidence)-pessimism (underconfidence) as an index on the unit interval, alpha E[0, 1]. Keynes introduces, in 1936 in his *General Theory*, additional informal concepts aimed at allowing a decisionmaker to deal with ambiguity (uncertainty). These concepts are *liquidity preference*, and *animal spirits*. Ellsberg (2001) does not deal at all with Keynes' GT and hence overlooks these additional elements in Keynes' analysis of decision making. A third concept added by Keynes, *conventions* or rules of thumb, will not be discussed here. Keynes did not formally model his optimism-pessimism variable, which he called animal spirits. Keynes pointed out that the solution for ambiguity averse decision makers was increased liquidity preference. Thus, for a fixed value of rho or w, decision makers can be more or less confident. Overconfidence leads to decreased liquidity preference while under-confidence leads to increased liquidity preference. The resort to very high discount rates applied to the future stream of expected cash flows from an investment in physical capital is discussed in Brady's 1987 *Synthese* article. The Hurwicz index ä is easily integrated formally into Keynes' c coefficient. In my 1994 article in *The International Studies in the Philosophy of Science*, I suggested augmenting Keynes' analysis by integrating lambda, 0< lambda <1, where lambda measures the skills, training, and knowledge of the decision maker. Thus, as lambda approaches 1, the decision maker can become overconfident. As lambda approaches 0, the decision maker can become under-confident.

Formally, Keynes' decision criteria becomes

Max lambda cA

References

Boole, G. (1954). The Laws of Thought. England: Dover.

Ellsberg, Daniel. (2001). Risk, Ambiguity, and Decision. New York: Garland

Machina, Mark. (2001). "Further Readings on Choice Under Uncertainty, Beliefs and the Ellsberg Paradox", in Ellsberg, ibid, pp. XXXIX-XLVIII.

Levi, Issac. (2001). "Introduction", in Ellsberg, ibid., pp. IX-XXXVII.

Keynes, J.M. (1921). A Treatise on Probability. London: Macmillan (AMS Reprinted, 1979).

Hailparin, T. (1965). "Best Possible Inequalities for the Probability of a Logical Function of Events". American Mathematical Monthly, 77, 343-359.

_____(1976). Boole's Logic and Probability. North Holland, Amsterdam.

Kampke, T. (1995). "Probabilistic Logic via Capacities". International Journal of Intelligent Systems, 10, 857-869.

Printed in the United States
67596LVS00002B/110

9 781413 472042